WONDERS OF THE WORLD

Endpapers: *One effect of erosion: the Totem Pole (right), one of the isolated pinnacles in Monument Valley on the Utah-Arizona border.*

Above: *A photomicrograph, taken with polarized light, of the crystal formation of salicine, the base of aspirin.*

Overleaf: *Antarctic wastes.*

ARTUS

WONDERS OF THE WORLD

Ronald W Clark

Copyright © Ronald W. Clark 1980

First published in 1980 by
Artus Publishing Company Ltd
91 Clapham High Street
London SW4 7TA

Colour separations by Newsele Litho Ltd
Filmset by Keyspools Ltd, Golborne, Lancs.
Printed by L.E.G.O., Vicenza, Italy

NATURAL WONDERS

These pages: The wonder of ultra-fast photography. The sequence of a drop of water hitting the surface is frozen at several of its stages.

Overleaf: The rolling dunes of the Sahara Desert.

CONTENTS

NATURAL WONDERS

The Grand Canyon

When Lt Joseph Ives, sent by the US War Department on a journey of discovery, reached the Colorado River as it rushed through the Grand Canyon of Arizona, he commented: 'Ours has been the first, and doubtless will be the last party of whites to visit this profitless locality. It seems intended by nature that the Colorado River, along the greater portion of its lonely and majestic way, shall be forever unvisited and undisturbed.' That was in the mid-nineteenth century; today more than 1,500,000 visitors annually gaze in awe at what is one of the most spectacular wonders of the natural world – 'a natural wonder which, so far as I know, is in kind absolutely unparalleled' as President Theodore Roosevelt said in 1903.

Standing on one rim of the canyon, the visitor looks across a gulf more than a mile deep. At the bottom can be seen the silver thread of the Colorado River which over millions of years has carved out the path along which its waters now rush – carrying daily up to half a million tons of material which is still carving an even deeper route for the river. On the far side of the canyon can be seen the towering walls rising to the opposite rim, anything from four to 18 miles away.

The scenic attraction of the Grand Canyon lies in the multi-coloured walls rising in layers some 1,500 metres (5,000 ft) from the river-bed, in the sinuous bends of the river itself, and in the complex system of peaks and buttes (isolated, steep-sided, flat-topped hills), minor canyons and gorges, and river-tributaries making up the whole system. Quite as fascinating to the geologist is the record of the rocks which reveal in a unique way the history of the earth from the rocks of the Archaean era of more than 500 million years ago to those of the Permian era of between 120 and 190 million years ago.

The first attempt to reach the bottom of the gorge was made by three Spanish horsemen in 1540, when the Spaniards were extending their conquests in what was to become the United States. They tried for many days to find a way down the steep slopes, managed to get some 460 metres (1,500 ft) down, but gave up when they realized that what they had taken to be pinnacles no bigger than a man were taller than church spires. When the opening-up of the West was begun by Americans in the early nineteenth century, trappers were no more successful. But after Ives had reached the river others followed and between 1869 and 1872 Major John Wesley Powell successfully explored virtually the whole course of the river through the gorge. Today the north and south rims of the canyon are followed by roads, and there are numerous mule-routes and paths from the rims to the river.

Below: *The Colorado River twisting through the Grand Canyon and* (right) *a view across the canyon showing, centre, one of the buttes.*

Niagara Falls

The world's most famous waterfall is known for its amazing spectacle rather than for breaking records for height or volume. Its waters drop about 55 metres (180 ft) – the exact height of the fall depending on conditions – compared with the 975 metres (3,200 ft) of Angel Falls in the jungles of Venezuela. Its flow in cubic metres per second is only a fraction of the amount tumbling over the Guayra Falls in Brazil. Yet despite this the mass of water passing over Niagara, first described in 1678 by the Jesuit Father Louis Hennepin who reported the Falls to be 600 feet (183 metres) high, is a sight unequalled anywhere in the world. Oscar Wilde is among the small number who have tried to denigrate the spectacle of Niagara. 'Every American bride is taken to Niagara Falls', he wrote, 'and the sight of this stupendous waterfall must be one of the earliest, if not the keenest, disappointments in married life.' Few have agreed. Some 12,000,000 people visit it yearly.

The Niagara River, which forms part of the frontier between Canada and the United States, runs from Lake Erie into Lake Ontario. Some 20 miles from its source, where it is divided into two by Goat Island, it drops over a rocky escarpment, the right-hand branch forming Niagara's 305-metre (1,000-ft) wide American Falls, and the left-hand branch forming the 783-metre (2,600-ft) horseshoe of Niagara's Canadian Falls.

'There is no actual harm in making Niagara a background whereon to display one's marvellous insignificance in a strong light,' said Mark Twain, 'but it requires a sort of superhuman self-complacency to enable one to do it.'

The Falls are produced by the geological formation of the area, which consists of an upper layer of hard dolomitic limestone covering a layer of softer shale. The softer material is easily worn away, with the result that the waters are constantly falling perpendicularly from an over-hanging edge, one of the most spectacular features of the falls. From time to time the undercut upper layer breaks away, so that over the centuries the falls have been moving upstream. About 12,000 years ago they were some seven miles nearer Lake Ontario and earlier this century it was estimated that they were still moving back at the rate of about a yard (0·9 metres) a year. Since 1950, however, there have been major diversions of the upper Niagara River and the water has been channelled off along four huge tunnels to hydro-electric stations. In addition, special control works have been built to spread the flow of water more evenly over the horseshoe falls. This has decreased erosion which may now be little more than 25 mm (1 in) a year.

Great efforts have been made by both the Canadian and the American authorities to preserve the attractions of Niagara. It has been agreed that a certain minimum flow must be kept despite hydro-electric schemes; and in 1969 the flow over the American Falls was diverted so that cemen-ting of the bedrock would further lessen erosion.

Over the years Niagara's attractions have been increased by the building of tunnels to important viewpoints at the side of the falls, by floodlighting at night and by the construction of observation towers. A footbridge leads from the American shore to Goat Island and a lift has been built there to take visitors to the Cave of the Winds, a viewpoint actually behind the falling waters.

Niagara has been the scene of spectacular sights since 1837 when the steamer *Caroline*, used to supply Canadian rebels, was set on fire above the falls by the Canadian authorities and then, blazing hard, was allowed to crash over them. On 30 June 1859 Charles Blondin – real name Jean François Gravelet – crossed the falls on a tightrope in five minutes, watched by 25,000 spectators. Four days later he repeated the performance but blindfolded and trundling a wheelbarrow. The following month he made a third tightrope crossing, this time with a man on his shoulders. And in September, in the presence of the Prince of Wales, later Edward VII, he made the crossing on stilts. A number of men and women have shot the falls in a barrel and some have survived, one of the first being Mrs Anna Taylor in 1901.

Opposite: *The American Falls in late March and* (below) *the horseshoe of the Canadian Falls.*

The Amazon

The greatest river-system in the world, the Amazon and its tributaries drain about 2,500,000 square miles – an area two-thirds as big as Europe – include 25,000 miles of navigable waters, and pour into the Atlantic Ocean three billion gallons of water a minute. Some 200 miles wide at its mouth, where it encloses an island the size of Switzerland, the river is unique in its geographical importance and in statistics which distinguish it from the rest of the world's rivers. The huge volume of its fresh, if muddy, waters can be recognized 200 miles from shore among the salt waters of the Atlantic; the ocean's tides can be felt and seen more than 500 miles up-river from its mouth.

The Amazon rises in the Andes only about 100 miles from the shores of the Pacific Ocean. There are different views as to which of its upper tributaries leads to the real source, but it is generally accepted that the river, known by a variety of names in its upper stretches, runs for nearly 4,000 miles mostly through Brazil before pouring its waters into the Atlantic north of the Equator.

It was from Quito, in the Ecuadorian Andes, that the first complete descent of the Amazon was made in 1541. A Spanish expedition under Gonzalo Pizarro – who had sailed with Columbus on the voyage which discovered America – had set out to find El Dorado, the fabled city where the houses were made of gold. The Spaniards, and the 4,000 Indian slaves who served as carriers, moved down along the head-waters of the Amazon into the jungles of the apparently limitless tropical forests. The expedition was faced with starvation but Francisco de Orellana offered to push on down-river in search of supplies. He never returned to the expedition, and whether he ever intended to is still unknown. Eight months later Orellana and his small band appeared on the shores of the Atlantic, with stories of 'the Amazons', women warriors who they claimed had attacked them and after whom they named the great river. Nearly a century passed before a Portuguese expedition in 1637 made the first journey the other way – up the river to its source. And it was only in the mid-nineteenth century that the Victorian naturalists Alfred Wallace and Henry Bates

began scientific exploration of the Amazon.

The greater part of the Amazon Basin is covered by rain-forest, the thick green carpet as it appears from the air, which contains a variety of plant life unequalled anywhere in the globe – and immense numbers of animals, birds, insects and fish. Typically, Henry Bates collected 8,000 different species of insects around one single centre.

Even today there is no bridge across the Amazon for the whole of its course. Yet the great river-basin has been opened up to an extent which would have astounded the early explorers. Until 1866 it had been open only to Brazilian and Peruvian ships. In that year, following a visit to Brazil by the scientist Louis Agassiz, and the interest taken in his work by the Emperor Dom Pedro II, the Amazon and a number of its more important tributaries – of which there are 1,000 – were thrown open to the shipping of the world.

Rubber was the first attraction and during the second half of the last century traders increasingly tapped the Amazon Basin's huge supplies, with 7,000-ton freighters steaming more than 2,000 miles up-river to the town of Iquitos to collect the precious cargo. With the increase of plantation rubber from Malaysia in the present century, the importance of the Amazon's rubber declined, but the gap has been partially closed by the discovery of manganese and other mineral wealth which is being utilized by the booming state of Brazil.

The most important factor in changing the prospects of the Amazon Basin during the last half-century has been the develop-ment of air transport. Landing strips have been hacked in the impenetrable jungle and communities whose only link with the outside world had been by slow and dangerous river transport are now in touch with the thriving cities on the coast.

In the league table of rivers, the Amazon has a discharge (118,931 cubic metres or 4,200,000 cu ft per second) three times that of its nearest rival, the Congo, and drains an area almost twice that of the Congo. Only in length does it fail to come first: the Nile is generally taken as being some 200 miles longer.

Two aerial views of the Amazon show (below) the river at Manaus and (opposite) the thick green carpet of the rain forest which contains a unique collection of plant life.

Antarctica

Antarctica, a continent which contains 90 per cent of the world's ice, is the only area on the globe covered by a Treaty whose signatories agree that it shall be used only for peaceful purposes and primarily for international scientific co-operation. Signed in 1959 and operative for 30 years, the Treaty has given a unique status to what was already a remarkable part of the world. Covering 5,400,000 square miles – the area of the United States and Mexico combined – Antarctica is not only ringed by a protecting barrier of pack-ice which made approach perilous until the age of the aeroplane, but is more remote than is generally realized. The nearest land, the tip of South America, is 600 miles away; New Zealand is 2,100 miles distant and South Africa 2,500. Combined with the climate, which on the central Antarctic plateau produces temperatures as low as $-88°C$ ($-126°F$) the continent's geographical position has made it one of the most inaccessible parts of the world.

In ancient times the Greeks called the area around the North Pole the Arctic, after the Greek word for 'Bear', the constellation of stars which rotated around the North Polar regions. Thus the great southern continent which it was believed must exist, naturally became known as the Antarctic, or the opposite of the Arctic.

Exploration is usually dated from the circumnavigation of the antarctic circle by Captain Cook in 1772–5. His reports of whales and seals attracted the traders but it was nearly half a century before serious exploration was begun – by the Russian Thaddeus von Bellingshausen, by the Scots-

man James Weddell, himself a sealer, and then by three nationally organized expeditions under Frenchman Dumont d'Urville, American Charles Wilkes and Englishman Sir James Clark Ross. These men and their successors in the nineteenth century were able to do no more than probe the outer defences of an inhospitable and apparently barren land, so that as late as 1895 the Sixth International Geographical Congress was able to resolve in London that 'the exploration of the Antarctic regions is the greatest piece of geographical exploration still to be undertaken.'

By the turn of the century the heroic age of antarctic exploration had begun. Scott and Shackleton are the best-known of the British explorers who slowly began to map and penetrate the icy wastes, moving inland from simple bases constructed on the perimeter and finding unexpected mountain ranges which stood up from the central antarctic plateau and were later found to rise in the Sentinel Range to 5,139 metres (16,860 ft). Preliminary soundings were taken of the great ice-sheet covering the continent, later found to be between 2,135 and 2,440 metres (7,000 and 8,000 ft) thick.

There was, naturally enough, a great competition to be first at the South Pole. It was won by the Norwegian Roald Amundsen who reached it in mid-December 1911. Scott, making his second journey to Antarctica, perished with the rest of his main party on the return trek. During the interwar years the *Discovery*, Scott's old ship, made more than a dozen voyages to Antarctica and opened the era of modern scientific investigation. The greatest change was brought about by the use of survey aircraft. The American Richard Byrd flew across the South Pole in 1929 and six

years later the American Lincoln Ellsworth made the first complete crossing of the continent by air.

Many other nations sent ships and men to the Antarctic and within a few years of the end of the Second World War the continent was dotted with bases from which groups investigated meteorology, glaciology and oceanography. In 1950 an International Geophysical Year (IGY) was organized for 1957–8, and in 1954 it was

agreed that observations should be concentrated on outer space and Antarctica – two areas where the advanced technology born out of the war could be used with the greatest effect. Nearly 60 stations were set up in the continent by the dozen nations which had agreed a plan of work. During the IGY the British Commonwealth Trans-Antarctic Expedition successfully carried out Shackleton's scheme which had been frustrated roughly 40 years earlier: the land crossing of Antarctica from the Weddell Sea to the Ross Sea.

So great was the success of the IGY that it was agreed to continue international co-operation. The outcome was the Antarctic Treaty, finally ratified on 23 June 1961. Signed by the 12 IGY nations – and later by Poland, Czechoslovakia, Denmark and the Netherlands – it froze all national claims to the continent for the 30 years and reserved the area for peaceful scientific purposes.

Top left: *A ski-fitted aircraft, one of the planes which have transformed exploration of the Antarctic and* (above) *an iceberg on the fringe of Antarctica.*

The Sahara

Snow in the Sahara is merely one of the surprises offered by the largest desert in the world. An area of more than three million square miles, stretching for almost 3,000 miles across North Africa from the Atlantic to the Red Sea, the Sahara is divided into north, central and southern divsions, while to the west it is known as the Atlantic Sahara and on the east it is usually called the Libyan desert. On the south the true desert changes gradually into steppes, savannahs, parklands and finally forest but on the other three sides the boundaries are more clearly defined. Morocco, Algeria, Tunisia, Libya, and the northern parts of Niger and Chad today control parts of the Sahara but the influence of the French, largely responsible for opening it up in the nineteenth century, is still strong. In 1960, two years before Algeria gained independence, France exploded her first atomic bomb in the Sahara near Reggane, 600 miles south of Oran.

While huge areas of the Sahara – an Arabic word for 'wilderness' – fit the popular idea of a desert and consist of mile after mile of rolling sand-dunes, there are many exceptions to this well-known picture. Among them are the Ahaggar mountains, a group of dramatic rock-peaks midway between the Atlantic and the Bight of Benin. They rise to 3,002 metres (9,850 ft) in the Tahat Peak, whose summit often carries snow for part of the year, and for the last three decades have increasingly been the goal of European climbing expeditions, notably those from France. Another exception to the popular idea of a desert is provided by the lines of fertile oases lying east-west across the Sahara and for long the staging-points of the caravan-trails which criss-crossed the waterless areas.

The character of the desert is largely governed by two factors. One is the low rainfall, which at some places is as little as 8·5 mm ($\frac{1}{3}$ in) a year. The other is the great variation in temperature, which can be as high as 38°C (100°F) during the day and as low as freezing-point at night. This variation builds up pressures within the rocks, and breaks them up into ever smaller fragments which eventually become sand.

The climate was once very different from what it is today and archaeologists who have studied the area during the last three decades have found in caves not only rock-drawings of elephants, lions and giraffes but the skeletons of animals which give proof that within comparatively recent – although pre-historic – times the climate must have supported considerable vegetation.

Many plans have been put forward for making the Sahara a fertile area once again. They have included the digging of artesian wells and the flooding of certain areas with desalinated sea-water. None of the ideas has so far been shown to be practicable. Meanwhile, the whole character of the Sahara is beginning to change, partly due to efforts to exploit its considerable oil deposits. Output is being steadily expanded, much of it coming from Hassi Massaoud whence it is pumped 400 miles to Bougie on the Mediterranean coast.

Opposite: A scene in the Algerian section of the Sahara and (below) in the salt deposits of the largest desert in the world.

Surtsey

In the autumn of 1963, astounded human beings looked on as an island was created from the depths of the sea off the south-west coast of Iceland. The Icelanders called it Surtsey after Surtur, the black god of fire in Norse mythology. Since those exciting days when flame, smoke and ashes shot up out of the ocean, scientists have been using Surtsey as a unique laboratory to discover how a new island, devoid of all life, is colonized by animals, plants and other living organisms.

On 6 November 1963 the seismograph in the Icelandic capital of Reykjavik recorded a slight tremor. Little notice was taken since Iceland is traversed by the Mid-Atlantic ridge, a belt running from Jan Meyen island in the Arctic, through Iceland, the Azores and the island of Tristan da Cunha to the Antarctic. Volcanic eruptions have occurred frequently along this belt – in 1946 and 1961 in Iceland, the Azores in 1957, Tristan da Cunha in 1961 and Jan Meyen in 1970. But something more unusual and spectacular took place in 1963.

On the 6th a fissure had opened up in the sea-bed beyond the western tip of the Westman Islands, a small group 20 miles off the mainland of Iceland. Soon after dawn eight days later a black cloud of smoke shot through with flame and surrounded by huge masses of ash and cinders was seen rising from the waters. A fishing boat, whose crew watched the extraordinary sight, and who found that the sea was two degrees warmer than normal, reported back by radio that a marine volcanic eruption was taking place.

Later measurements showed that by this time large quantities of cinders and lava were being thrown up from a quarter-mile chasm in the bed of the sea nearly 122 metres (400 ft) below the waves. By the following day the cone of erupted material on the sea-bed was breaking the surface of the sea and the new island was being born. From the air Surtsey presented an amazing spectacle with the lava constantly adding to the size of the island and clouds of steam rising from the points where the glowing lava touched the water.

By 20 November the highest point on Surtsey's cone was about 70 metres (230 ft) above the waves and by the first weeks of 1964 it was double that height. Early in February a second cone appeared on the island and immediately began throwing out more material. Throughout the next few months stormy weather whipped up the waves and sea-water was thrown crashing down the cones, causing heavy explosions in the heart of the volcano which sent masses of cinders into the air. Thus for weeks sea and storm fought a constant battle with the fire and flame below; but the steadily increasing land slowly gained the upper hand and soon after the end of 1964 Surtsey's future was assured. Later in 1965 two minor eruptions in the waters around the new island produced small islets, both of which were soon overcome by the sea, leaving only Surtsey.

The island was now the southernmost extension of Iceland and thus the first landfall met by birds migrating from Europe in the spring and many species were soon found on the island. So were plants, some 40 species of which were growing on Surtsey by 1972. Since then the island that men watched rise from the waves has been an increasingly important research site for biologists.

Below: *A volcanic eruption, Surtsey, 16 November 1963.*

Carlsbad Caverns

One evening in 1901 Jim White, a young miner trying his luck in the far west of the United States, was intrigued by the sight of millions of bats emerging from a New Mexico hillside in their regular search for insects. Investigating the cave-mouth from which they came, he found immense deposits of bat guano, a nitrate-rich fertilizer. Quite as important, he had stumbled across the greatest underground labyrinth in the world, a system of caves and tunnels which is today known to extend for at least 23 miles and may extend for many more.

Near the entrance to the huge system, outside Carlsbad in New Mexico, and 100 miles south-east of where the Americans tested the world's first nuclear weapon in the summer of 1945, there have been found circular rock cooking pits and grinding bowls. These signs of early occupation are supported by paintings or pictographs on the rock walls, but it is unlikely that the native Indians ventured far into the intimidating network of passages and halls. The Spanish conquistadors who passed through the area in the fifteenth century do not mention the caverns, and the first record of their existence comes in the records of the cattlemen who settled in the area in the 1880s.

However, it was Jim White who led the way for exploration of the amazing system.

Produced very largely by the dissolving action of water working its way through the limestone, the more important of the Carlsbad Caverns are as much as 335 metres (1,100 ft) below ground. The biggest of the caverns so far discovered is the suitably named Big Room, about 400 metres long, 200 metres wide and 95 metres high (1,300 × 650 × 300 ft). Like many of the other caves, the Big Room holds an impressive display of stalagmites and stalactites, including the Giant which is more than 18 metres (60 ft) tall. The King's Palace, the Queen's Room and the Green Lake Room are other chambers which are today open to the public who are taken down by a lift.

White quickly became an unofficial guide. Then, as the fame of the caverns

grew, he was appointed a Park Ranger by the National Parks Service. The extraordinary scenic beauty of the underground labyrinth so impressed President Coolidge that in 1923 he declared the area to be the Carlsbad Cave National Monument.

Soon afterwards the National Geographical Society organized a series of extensive scientific explorations of the caves and this in turn resulted in the area being turned into a National Park, which now extends to more than 18,555 hectares (45,846 acres) of federally-owned land.

Above: *Inside the greatest underground labyrinth in the world. There are three layers in the Carlsbad Caverns system, one 229 metres (750 ft) below ground, one 274 metres (900 ft) down and one at 335 metres (1,100 ft).*

Yellowstone National Park

The scalding waters of Old Faithful, regularly surging up more than 60 metres (200 ft) from the depths of the earth, provide the most spectacular sight in the Yellowstone National Park, the first national park to be created (in 1872) anywhere in the world. Some 60 by 50 miles, it is 90 per cent forested and consists mainly of a volcanic plateau between 2,130 and 2,590 metres (7,000 and 8,500 ft) high.

Iceland, from whose language the English took the word 'geyser', meaning to gush, has its own hot geysers and springs; so has New Zealand. But within the Yellowstone Park – most of it in the State of Wyoming – with its total of more than 200 geysers and up to 10,000 hot springs, there are more of these extraordinary features than in the whole of Iceland and New Zealand combined.

Although part of the Yellowstone site was included in the Louisiana Purchase of 1803, it was only four or five years later that John Colter became the first white man to visit the area. Another quarter century passed before details of the amazing sights to be seen in the Yellowstone became

known through an article in the *Philadelphia Gazette*. These include magnificent mountains and the Obsidian Cliff of black glass from which the Indians once carved their arrow-heads. Across the south-west corner runs the Continental Divide, the waters on one side flowing into the Pacific, those on the other into the Atlantic.

But the geysers have always provided the main spectacle. Some perform very regularly. Thus Old Faithful spouts, on average, once every 65 minutes and does so for from two-and-a-half to five minutes. Others are unpredictable, while yet others perform as frequently as every few minutes (but with much smaller output) or every few days, weeks or months. Among these is

Giant Geyser, which throws out more water than any of its rivals. After an interval varying from nine to 21 days, Giant Geyser performs for one-and-a-half hours, throwing out 700,000 gallons of water; about 22 tons of water is estimated to be in the air at any one moment during the display.

The machinery by which all geysers work is much the same despite their variation of performance. They occur where the extreme temperatures in the earth's crust are comparatively close to the surface. Water seeping down into the ground collects near these hot spots in the geyser's plumbing system and is turned into steam. This steam expands and forces upwards the cooler water lying above it. Constrictions in the system hold back this water until a sudden burst of pressure from the build-up below sends it jetting up into the air. As the geyser is thus clearing itself the water, cooled, falls back on the surface and eventually seeps down to the hotter depths and then the cycle is repeated.

Other hot water phenomena in Yellowstone include bubbling hot springs, which are really small geysers, coloured hot springs, and small bubbling mud volcanoes. There are also fossil forests, popularly known as petrified forests. These were formed long ago when volcanoes belched out clouds of volcanic dust which settled on the trees. Water carrying silica from the volcanic ash seeped through this dust into the trees. The wood itself then dissolved and was replaced by the silica which today forms a reproduction in rock of the original trees. In places a succession of up to a dozen such 'forests' can be seen, showing that after periods of eruption there intervened quiescent years during which a fresh generation of trees grew up.

Opposite: *Old Faithful, the famous hot geyser of Yellowstone National Park, sends its scalding waters some 61 metres (200 ft) up into the air.*

Above: *One of the mammoth hot springs for which the Park is also famous.*

Ayers Rock

In 1873 the explorer William C. Gosse, travelling through the flat outback of Northern Australia, saw ahead of him the outline of a hill where a hill had no right to be. 'When I was only two miles distant', he later wrote, 'and the hill for the first time coming into view, what was my astonishment to find it was an immense pebble rising abruptly from the plain. This rock is certainly the most wonderful natural feature I have seen.' This biggest rock in the world, an immense boulder more than five miles around and rising nearly 350 metres (1,150 ft) from the surrounding desert, was eventually named Ayers Rock after a premier of South Australia.

Lying 250 miles south-west of Alice Springs, it today forms part of a National Park and Wildlife Sanctuary that also includes two other remarkable giant outcrops; Mount Olga 25 miles to the west, a collection of round-topped summits; and

Coon Butte Crater

Some 20 miles west of Winslow, Arizona, the undulating plains are indented with a huge bowl-shaped crater, three-quarters of a mile across. Its rim rises for some 60 metres (200 ft) from the surrounding country, and from its top the sides of the crater plunge for 183 metres (600 ft) to the rough crater floor. This is Coon Butte, also known as Crater Mound, the end product of a giant meteorite which struck the earth thousands of years ago and one of the most impressive examples of what can happen when a large meteor enters the earth's atmosphere.

Every day many million meteors arrive from outer space. The vast majority of them are small, become incandescent due to friction with the atmosphere, and burn up completely as 'shooting stars'. Those big enough to survive fall as meteorites, all of them still small by comparison with the giant which hit the earth at Coon Butte.

No one is sure when the huge specimen fell, but a date of about 50,000 years ago is often accepted. The late Sir Richard Gregory, former editor of *Nature*, thought that it landed in historical times and once said: 'If we had come into contact with a large collection of such solid masses instead of one or a few the earth would have been reduced to the dead condition of the moon upon which thousands of similar craters are visible.'

For miles around the crater the ground is covered with nickel-iron fragments. Some

are chip size, others are huge blocks weighing hundreds of pounds and it has been claimed that small diamonds have been found in some of them.

The Coon Butte meteorite is believed to have struck the earth from the north and to have produced a crater which was originally between 335 and 365 metres (1,100 and 1,200 ft) deep. Boring operations were begun in the centre of the crater in 1906 and later transferred to the southern rim. It was here, in 1922, that drilling was brought to a halt when the drill struck, at nearly 425 metres (1,400 ft), what was believed to be a huge mass of meteoric iron.

In 1960 further confirmation of the crater's origin was given when coesite was found among the sands of the crater's floor. This is a form of silica which had never before been found in nature; but it had been created in the laboratory. Experiments had then shown that its production needed enormously high temperatures and pressures – just the conditions created by impact with the earth of an enormous mass heated by its passage through the earth's atmosphere.

Above: *The giant meteorite crater, Coon Butte.*

the flat-topped Mount Connor, 50 miles to the east. Neither is comparable to the immense looming mass of Ayers Rock that is seen from the desert when approached along the single road, sometimes impassable due to flash-floods.

Ayers Rock is composed of a hard sandstone, red-brown in colour but bright red when seen in the light of the setting sun. Gosse and his Afghan camel-driver climbed the rock and from the top were able to see Mount Olga and Mount Connor, which like Ayers Rock were eroded some 500 million years ago from a mountain range after the desert from which they now rise was covered by the sea. After the sea had disappeared, the red rocks were contorted and folded back on themselves, then finally eroded to leave only the pockets of slightly harder material which exist as today's giant protruberances.

Deep vertical fissures run for hundreds of feet up the surface in many places. The most famous of these has left a giant slab, known as the Kangaroo's Tail, lying almost separate from the main body of the rock.

These fissures are due to weaknesses in the rock and have steadily been deepened by the rush of water that pours off after heavy rainfall. These storms turn the fissures themselves into spectacular waterfalls that cease as suddenly as they begin.

The lower slopes are cut into by natural caves that were for years the home of aborigines who have ornamented the walls with rock paintings. The Pitjandara tribes who have for long held their religious ceremonies around the base of the Rock have invested every feature of it with special names and significance. It was, they maintain, created in the Dreamtime, the southern face during a battle between the poisonous snakes and the carpet snakes, the northern face by the hare wallabies.

These legends have had their effect on later explorers as Charles Mountford made clear after the Second World War. 'When I saw Ayers Rock some years previously I was almost overawed by its size, its colour, its silence and its solitude, and in retrospect these were my only memories,' he wrote. 'But later, when I learned the legends of the place, of the snakes which fought round

the Mutigulana waterhole, of the Marsupial Rats and the evil Kalpunya, of the distraught Lizard and its lost boomerang, and of the harmless Marsupial Mole, my outlook changed. The immense and beautiful surroundings were no longer mere precipices, caves or splashes of colour; they had been vitalized by the stories that the aborigines had told me; the precipices were the work of the little Lizard or the Marsupial Rats, the caves the one-time camping places of ancestral beings, and the grey smudge on the cliff the smoke-stain from the burning camp of the Sleepy-Lizard women.'

Above: *The spectacle of the colour changes of Ayers Rock. The rock is composed of quartz and feldspar, cemented by brown and red oxides of iron and some magnetite. The colours alter according to the strength of the light and the changing seasons.*

Mount Everest

In 1852 a Bengali mathematician rushed into the office of the Surveyor-General of India, Sir Andrew Waugh, and exclaimed: 'Sir, I have discovered the highest mountain in the world!' From the field observations of a survey team, he had worked out the height of Peak XV in the great range of the Himalayas which bounds India on the north-east and had discovered that the average of six separate readings came to 29,002 feet (8,836 metres). This was far higher than any mountain whose height had been measured and Sir Andrew named the peak after his predecessor, Sir George Everest. Contemporary measurements give the height as 29,145 feet (8,880 metres).

Mount Everest, which can be seen from many parts of north-east India, lies on the frontier between Tibet and Nepal. These two countries stopped entry by foreigners for many years, and it was only early in the twentieth century that negotiations were begun for a British attempt to climb the mountain. These were halted – partly by the start of the First World War – but in 1921 an expedition set out to reconnoitre the mountain. It was not yet known whether men could live at such heights without the use of oxygen, which at that date had to be carried in heavy metal cylinders, while even the surroundings of the mountain had not been mapped.

The approach marches had to be made across the high bleak plateau of Tibet. Then a way had to be found through the tangled crevasses of the miles-long East Rongbuk Glacier. Steep slopes of ice had to be climbed to a dip in the north-east ridge of Everest known as the North Col. Only then were the mountaineers able to see at close hand the long wind-swept north-east ridge that led to the summit, a ridge they were not then equipped to tackle.

In 1922 seven of the Sherpa porters carrying a fresh expedition's loads were swept to their deaths on the slopes of the North Col. In 1924 George Mallory, one of Britain's greatest mountaineers, and Andrew Irvine, disappeared on the upper slopes of the mountain. Whether they reached the summit before disaster overtook them has never been finally settled.

Other British attempts to climb Everest were made in the 1930s but it for long seemed that reaching such heights was beyond man's ability, even with the help of oxygen. Only in 1953 did the New Zealander Edmund (later Sir Edmund) Hillary and Sherpa Tenzing Norkay, members of a British party led by Brigadier (later Lord) Hunt, stand on the summit of Everest after reaching the mountain through Nepal.

The ascent of Everest had been helped

by improved oxygen equipment developed during the Second World War, and by much other specialized clothing and kit. The British success was followed by ascents of the mountain by Swiss, American, Italian, Polish, Indian, Chinese, Japanese and many other parties. Women have climbed Everest, and it has been climbed without oxygen.

The peak is the highest of many scores of great mountains in the Himalayas, a range which stretches about 1,500 miles, the distance between Moscow and London, from the Brahmaputra in the east to the bend of the Indus in the west; Kangchenjunga, Nanga Parbat, Makalu, Annapurna and Nanda Devi are some of the greatest. Beyond the Indus there rise the Karakoram, virtually an extension of the Himalayas and containing the second highest mountain in the world, K2, once known as Mount Godwin Austen. The Karakoram also have the world's longest glaciers outside the Antarctic.

Above: *John Evans in the Khumbu icefall on the approach to Everest and* (right) *the upper south-west face of Everest showing, left, the north ridge seen from Gokyo Ri.*

Weather Forecasting

The latest aid to forecasting whether it will rain or shine has an ancestry going back at least to the 1930s with the release of the first weather-balloons – known as radio-sondes – which automatically radioed information back to the ground. Before that, weather-forecasters had to rely on the ground-level observations taken by meteorological stations or by ships at sea. During the Second World War many operations depended on accurate forecasting. After the war, radar was used to plot the movements of rain-clouds, and automatic devices to transmit information on temperature, pressure and humidity, were dropped in uninhabited areas.

All this dealt only with conditions at relatively small heights. But it was realized that the earth's weather was conditioned by the circulation of the whole vast mass of air known as the atmosphere. Its higher reaches were first penetrated in the 1950s when meteorological rockets, adapted from the German V2 rockets which bombarded London, were used to make observations in the upper atmosphere.

The decisive change in weather-forecasting began in 1960 when the United States launched the first of its Tiros satellites. Circling the earth about 900 miles up, they transmitted a continuous picture of the world's cloud-cover. These sophisticated machines now provide extremely large masses of data which are fed into electronic computers. The extent to which the latest technological aids are now being used is shown by a typical international research operation mounted in 1974 to investigate the intertropical convergence zone which influences much of the world's weather. Scientists from 25 countries, a geostationary satellite, 38 ships, three weather ships, 13 aircraft, and 15 surface and three radiosonde stations were all involved.

Forecasts vary from those which predict weather for the next day to those which suggest what it will be like a month or so ahead. The shorter the forecast the greater the chance of accuracy; but meteorologists normally stress that their work is based on the statistical chance of weather-patterns following those of previous years.

Above: *A satellite photograph of the large vortex of a typhoon in the south central Pacific Ocean.*

Stress Patterns in Metal

The patterns in which stresses build up in metals when they are put under load are today being revealed by methods developed from a discovery made in 1816 by the Scottish scientist, Sir David Brewster.

Brewster found that transparent materials under stress could exhibit coloured patterns if they were viewed with the use of polarized light – light whose waves had been restricted to certain directions of vibration. These patterns indicated where the stresses had built up. At the time, stress-distribution problems facing the engineers who constructed metal bridges, factories or machinery, were solved largely by mathematical analysis. Later this was to be supplemented by the use of strain-gauges. But theoretical work was not always satisfactory and, when the metal structures were complicated, involved an immense amount of calculation; the use of strain-gauges was also lengthy and costly. Thus it was clear that if Brewster's discovery could ever be adapted to engineering then immense benefits could follow.

Other nineteenth-century scientists worked on the subject – among them Fresnel, Clerk Maxwell and Mach – but glass was the only transparent material available, and the difficulty of cutting glass to the shape of even simple metal parts blocked development into the field of engineering.

The situation began to change in the twentieth century as first celluloid and then a whole range of transparent plastics such as Bakelite, Catalin and Araldite became available. By the 1930s it was possible to build a plastic model of the structure to be investigated, examine it under polarized light, observe the patterns which built up as the model was loaded, and then use the theory of elasticity to calculate the magnitudes and directions of the stresses in every

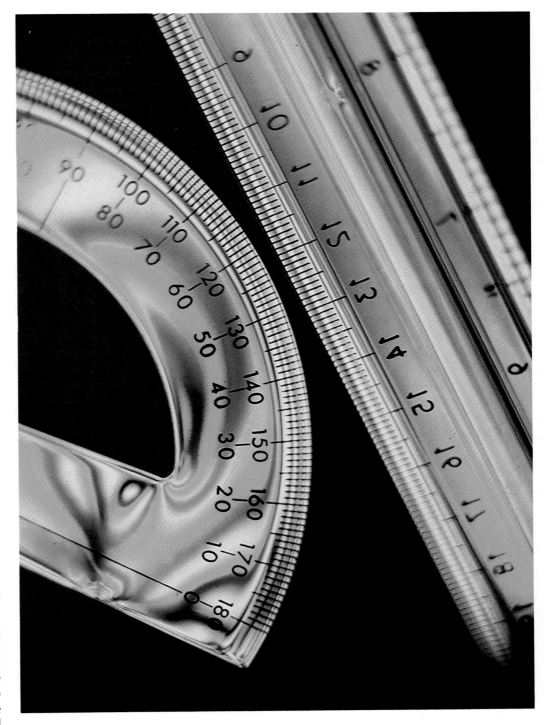

part of the model. It was then possible to deduce the stresses which would be set up in the structure itself if it were stressed in the same way. It was quickly found that the method was reliable, and it was successfully used to investigate the wheels and tyres of railway wagons, the teeth of gear wheels, roller bearings, and components for both ships and aircraft.

The method of photo-elastic analysis, as it was called, was found to be of particular use in dealing with complicated components and in evaluating the effect of making changes in existing parts. In many cases the mathematical work would have been very great indeed, and in some cases it would have been ineffective.

During more recent years a method has been developed which eliminates even the need for a plastic model. In this, a reflecting layer is first applied to the structure to be investigated. On this there is then superimposed a transparent coating having what is known as a large stress-optic constant. When the structure is put under load, the stresses built up in its surface layers are similar to those built up in the transparent coating. These are revealed by the use of polarized light which passes through the transparent coating, and is then reflected back through this coating for the second time by the first layer put on the structure.

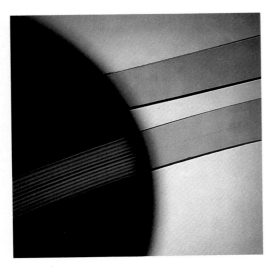

These photographs show how stress patterns appear in plastic models when photographed under polarized light. These patterns only occur when a metal or plastic is under stress; in the picture (top right) the top piece of clear plastic is straight, the bottom one bent. The protractor and rule (below) show the stress patterns produced during manufacture.

Erosion Effects

The most spectacular effects of erosion must be imagined rather than seen. The huge dome of chalk which once arched up from the North Downs of southern England and then curved over towards what are now the South Downs, has been worn away by erosion over millions of years to reveal the Sussex Weald. The land which once stretched from the Dover cliffs to Cap Gris Nez has been eroded by the forces of the sea which have created the English Channel separating England and France. In the north-west of Scotland the grey Lewisian gneiss, one of the oldest rocks in Britain, and one which long ago formed its own peaks and ranges, had been ground down to form the landscape of Sutherland from which its successor peaks of red sandstone rise.

Only in gorges and ravines is it possible to see evidence of how one form of erosion – that of rivers – has done its work over countless eons by wearing away the rock over which the river flows. The most

spectacular example of all is that of the Colorado River in Arizona where the river, deepening the Grand Canyon by 15 cm (6 in) a century, has taken away an estimated 1,000 cubic miles of solid material.

Virtually all the world's landscape is the result of erosion which has been carving it into the shapes one sees today, and is still at work. Wind, rain, frost, glaciers, the running water of rivers, and the constantly-rolling breakers of the oceans all play their parts in thus making the landscape. Plants, whose roots help to break up solid rock, animals which denude the vegetational cover, and roads and railway cuttings, also play a role in the continuing process.

While wind and water wear down the surface of the earth, geological movements are taking place which create new ranges. A struggle between the two forces is always at work, and the age of mountain ranges can often be judged by the amount of weathering they have experienced since they were created. This weathering consists, basically, of a rounding of corners and sharp points: thus it is obvious that the Himalayas with their sharp and dramatic peaks are younger than the rounded summits of the Scottish Highlands, many of

which date back to the pre-Cambrian times of more than 500 million years ago.

The mechanisms by which erosion operates are many and varied. Rain does much of its work by collecting in fissures, then freezing, a process in which it expands by 10 per cent and thus tends to enlarge the fissures and cracks. Glaciers grind down the rocks over which they slowly move. And rivers, plus the force of gravity, are constantly moving the rock-debris down to lower levels.

Wind and rain together have produced many startling rock formations, including many of the logans, or rocking stones, which consist of rounded rocks so finely balanced that they can be made to move with little effort. Erosion has also accounted for the spectacular rock formations known as stacks – thin tall towers of rock which were once part of the British mainland but now stand isolated off the coast. In many parts of the world there are also isolated rocks which have been worn into fantastic shapes.

When major landscape changes take place they usually do so too slowly to be noticed in one life-time – or even within one century. But erosion of the soil itself

can be much quicker. Bad agricultural management can allow the effect of wind and rain to remove valuable top-soil in a very few years, the most famous example being that of the 'dust-bowl' in the Middle West of the United States where large areas were changed and ruined in the 1930s.

Today, another and very different kind of erosion is also at work – that of human beings. In the Cairngorm mountains of Scotland, near the summit of Snowdon in North Wales, and even on Silbury Hill, in Wiltshire, the passage of sightseers' feet has become a danger: so much so that special protective measures have been introduced to limit 'human erosion'.

Three forms of erosion.

Opposite above: The balancing rock, Salisbury, Zimbabwe, formed by the erosion of wind and rain.

Opposite below: An aerial photograph of the Badlands, United States, shows how erosion is consuming the old alluvial surface.

Below: Falaise de Bracquemont, near Dieppe, on the south side of the English Channel – itself produced by erosion of the chalk uplands which once linked England and France.

1

2

3

4

Crystal Growth

A crystal is a solid composed of atoms arranged in an orderly repetitive array, and a growing crystal provides a fascinating demonstration of how one group of substances is made. If, for instance, saltpetre is dissolved in boiling water and then poured on to a plate, small glassy needles will immediately begin to form all over the plate as the solution cools, coming into existence out of who knows where. If the solution of water and saltpetre is allowed a longer period of cooling-off the needles will take a longer time to form. But they will still have the same shape, an illustration of the fact that all crystals of the same substance build themselves up into similar patterns, whatever the circumstances of their birth and growth, and are in this way different from amorphous materials which have no definite shape or form. 'In every case,' wrote a Victorian scientist, 'the [atoms] are silently and symmetrically drawn together in accordance with the laws imposed upon them by the Creator, just as the bricklayer in building a wall places brick upon brick in the order which the architect has appointed.'

The speed at which this process goes on varies according to conditions, but it has been estimated that in some cases atoms line themselves up at the rate of 3,300 million million a second.

In earlier times it was thought that some crystals were the result of ice having frozen so hard that it would never thaw; in fact the Greek word for crystal is *krystallos* which comes from *kryos* meaning cold. Today it is known that the factors influencing the growth of crystals include temperature, pressure and chemical conditions and that they come into being by evaporation, cooling or reduction of pressure among other methods.

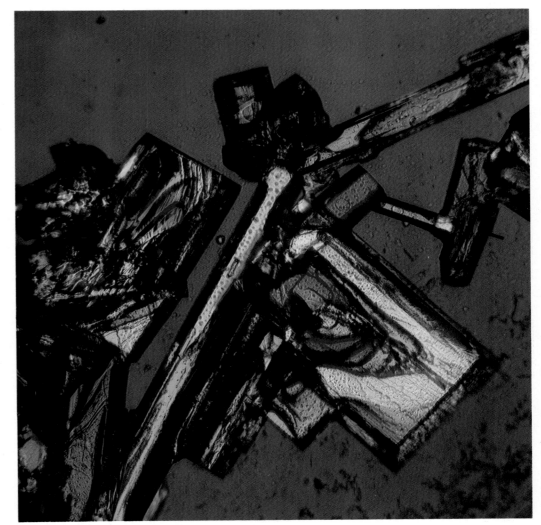

Left: *A series of four microphotographs showing the growth of vitamin C.*

Right above: *Crystals of Rochelle salt (potassium sodium tartrate), the salt used in the making of baking powder and Seidlitz powders.*

Right below: *Crystal formation of Epsom salts (magnesium sulphate) photographed under low magnification and polarized light.*

The Great Barrier Reef

The greatest coral reef in the world, 1,250 miles from end to end and covering 80,000 square miles – the area of England, Wales and Ireland – is a wonder-world of marine life lying off the east coast of Australia. The Great Barrier Reef, as it is called, was formed more than 10,000 years ago after the eastern side of the sub-continent, today the State of Queensland, slowly subsided for many hundreds of feet. The sea covered the land and in the shallow waters there began to be built up a complex series of ridges formed from the numberless skeletons of simple marine plants and animals.

These living things, whose dead remains are known as coral, flourish only in severely limited conditions. The water must be only 60–90 metres (200–300 ft) deep, its temperature must be between 18° and 35°C (65° and 95°F), and the water itself must be salt. The last requirement means that where the rivers of Australia pour out into the Pacific, their non-salty waters produce gaps in the main reef. This itself is a series of islands or cays, shingle ramparts from which the roar of the surf can always be heard, and sinuous convoluted channels. Interspersed among the maze of land and water are some rocky islands, the peaks of the area submerged thousands of years ago.

In the north, where the Great Barrier Reef begins at the Torres Strait, it is almost continuous and only between 20 and 30 miles off the mainland; further south the pattern of isles and islets is more complicated and as much as 200 miles off the coast. Nearly 350 different kinds of coral have gone to the making of the reef and bore-holes show that in places it is more than 150 metres (500 ft) thick. The dry land which has been formed as the millions of skeletons have been built up higher than the surface of the sea is infinitely varied; at some places it is just coral strand, at others it is thick with mangroves while on some islands there grow trees and vegetation

whose seeds have been carried from the mainland by birds.

The living coral – made up of the millions of minutely small creatures whose skeletal structure forms the reef – can with few exceptions be seen only at low tide. The marine life, which is claimed to be both bigger and more colourful on the reef than elsewhere and which is one of its great attractions, can be seen at all times in the clear surrounding waters. It includes multitudinous varieties of brightly-coloured sea-shells and giant clams which weigh many hundredweight and have myriads of eyes. There are sea-urchins, star-fish and anemones as large as dinner plates, all in abundance. Crawling across the coral there comes the bêche-de-mer, also known as the sea-cucumber or sea-slug, as thick as a man's wrist and much sought after as a delicacy. Sharks swim in the water as well as the ugly stone-fish, a foot-long creature from whose back protrude 13 razor-sharp spines carrying poisonous venom.

Twice a year huge green turtles can be seen waddling ashore to lay their eggs, while the reef is also the home of the increasingly rare dugong, a marine mammal that grows three metres (10 ft) long, carries its solitary young under its arm, has a peculiar feeble cry and is thought to be the origin of the mermaid legend.

The Great Barrier Reef today has simple accommodation for the tourists who come in growing numbers to study its extra-ordinary life. Efforts are increasing to protect this life, but in the long term the future rests on the outcome of a continuing battle with the elements. The simple coral life is constantly adding to the substance of the reef; this, in turn, is constantly being removed by wind and waves, by boring mussels, sponges, and other organisms that erode the material and eventually deposit it on the ocean floor.

Opposite: *Masthead Island, Capricorn Group, part of the Great Barrier Reef.*

Below: *Coral polyp, one of the colourful sights of the Reef and Clamon coral, one of the 350 kinds which have helped to make the reef.*

The Oldest Trees

The world's oldest living tree, for long thought to be one of the giant *Sequoia gigantea* growing on the slopes of the Californian Sierra, is now known to be a bristle-cone pine nearly 3,350 metres (11,000 ft) up on Wheeler's Peak in east Nevada. While the oldest living sequoia is thought to be about 3,500 years old, the bristle-cone easily holds the record with an estimated 4,900 years.

The key to dating with an accuracy that is only a few years out either way is the science of dendrochronology, which makes use of the growth rings which trees produce annually. These rings vary in size and character, as Leonardo da Vinci pointed out as long ago as the fifteenth century. It is known today that these differences are largely due to climate, and their study early in the present century was largely due to the work of an American astronomer trying to link sun-spots with climate.

Among the giant sequoia which had then been felled was one cut down in 1892. Its earliest ring was dated back to 1307 BC. It was estimated that it had sprouted about 1320 BC, thus giving it a life of about 3,212 years when brought down. Several other specimens were found to have more than 3,000 rings, and it was long accepted that those still standing were the oldest living trees on earth. One result of this longevity was their great height; a giant sequoia was known to have reached 84 metres (275 ft) and a *sequoia sempervivens* more than 107 metres (350 ft).

In 1953 dendrochronologists from the Laboratory of Tree-Ring Research in Tucson, Arizona, began investigating the bristle-cone pines in the Inya National Forest of the White Mountains to the east of the Sierra Nevada. This is an alpine that grows in western America, from 6–18 metres (20–60 ft) tall and between 0·3–0·6 metres (1·2–2·4 ft) in diameter. It does not flourish in Britain where the tallest specimen is believed to be a 9-metre (30-ft) tree at Warnham Court, Sussex. The scientists soon realized that they were dealing with trees that might be older than the sequoia, and in 1957 they found their first proof: a 4,000-plus tree, that further examination showed to be 4,600 years old. A few years later the even older specimen of the bristle-cone pine was found in Nevada.

While the tree seems likely to hold its record for a considerable time, experts point out that the sequoia may in the distant future win it back. This is because many of the giant sequoia now standing appear to be in the prime of life and could, it is claimed, be living in 3,000 years' time. However, the older bristle-cones are what have been called 'living ruins' and the *potential* life of the sequoia is thus seen as much longer.

Above: *Giant sequoia in Mariposa Grove, Yosemite National Park. The sequoia, long thought to be the oldest living tree, may regain that place when the bristle-cone pine (below) dies out.*

The Blue Whale

Larger than 30 elephants, weighing more than 2,000 people and even bigger than the extinct dinosaur, the Blue Whale is by far the largest mammal of all time.

Although often mistakenly thought of as a fish, the Blue Whale is, like all other members of the order of Cetacea – whales, dolphins and porpoises – a warm-blooded mammal that breathes through its lungs, suckles its young on milk, and although living in the ocean needs to take in regular draughts of air in order to survive. Like other whales, it is distinguished from fish by the blow-hole on the top of its head, the absence of gill openings and the horizontal position of its tail. Up to 119 tons in weight and up to 30 metres (100 ft) long, these enormous creatures can eat nothing larger than herring, and normally feed on masses of shrimp-like crustacea. Their method of doing so is to cruise just below the surface of the ocean with huge mouth wide open. Into this waiting maw there go gallons of water and a mass of sub-surface food. The food is trapped on the frayed edges of sheets of horny baleen – 'whalebone' – that hang from the upper jaws and the water is allowed to flow back to the sea. The solid food is then passed to the stomach where it is digested much as food is digested in other mammals. As much as a ton of 'krill', as the small crustaceans are called, has been found in the stomach of one whale.

At birth, a Blue Whale is about seven metres (23 ft) long and weighs about two tons. It quickly increases in size and becomes an adult after about two years. Thereafter it grows more slowly but soon reaches the full size which it keeps for its normal life-span of up to 20 years. Its heart will by this time weigh half a ton, its tongue a third of a ton, and some of its arteries will be so big that a child would be able to crawl through them.

The whale, being a mammal, cannot get dissolved oxygen from the water and it therefore has to get it from the air, the same as other land animals. This means that it has to make regular visits to the surface. It does this between dives which can last for up to 45 minutes. Under water, the whale holds its breath. Then, reaching the surface, it blows out from its nostrils a huge mass of oily foam – the 'spout' that is often believed to be a fount of water – and takes in breath before its next dive.

The huge animals, tinged with the blue cast that gives them their name, their undersides often sulphur-coloured with a film of diatoms which has produced the nickname 'sulphur-bottoms', normally 'cruise' at about six knots – roughly twice as fast as a person normally walks. They can double that speed for short periods. The comparatively slow speed, and huge size, have made the Blue Whale particularly vulnerable to attack and it has, like other whales which are in great danger of extinction, been protected for the last few years.

Another reason for the Blue Whale's vulnerability is its greater economic value than other whales, and not only on account of its size. Like other whales it has always been sought for the blubber or whale fat which is turned into whale oil, and the Blue Whale's is thicker than that of other species of Cetacea. The blubber is the whale's alternative to the covering of hair or fur which other mammals, warm-blooded as they are, need to keep their temperature constant under all conditions.

Such a covering would become water-logged on a whale and the problem is solved by the internal layer of blubber rather than an external layer of fur. The average yield of oil from the blubber of a Blue Whale was 70–80 barrels when it was hunted commercially, although it is on record that one specimen provided 305 barrels. So if whalers had the choice of attacking a Blue or another kind, it was the Blue which was attacked.

Today the remaining species of whale are in grave danger of extinction since a few countries, notably Japan and the Soviet Union, are mercilessly hunting and slaughtering them despite a world-wide moratorium.

Below: The mammoth Blue Whale, drawn to scale with a standard London double-decker bus, which is 8·4 metres (27·7 ft) long.

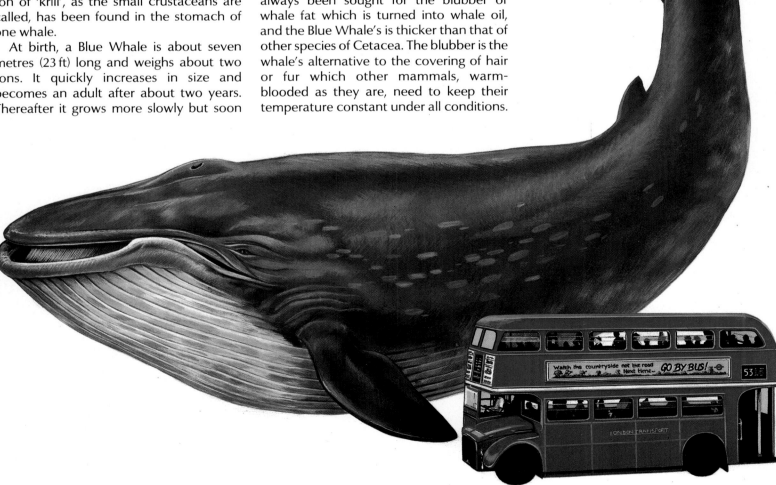

Camouflage and Mimicry

Animals – a word which the zoologist uses to describe mammals, birds, fishes and insects – evade attacks by predators and survive the seasonal changes of climate by a variety of ingenious methods.

Camouflage is one of the most common of them and can be observed by anyone who visits the northern hills of Britain in both summer and winter. During the summer the hare, the Arctic fox and the ptarmigan can sometimes be seen in their brown or grey coats or feathers – but not easily seen since they blend so well into the landscape. Six months later the same animals and birds are all in white, the camouflage which their fur or feathers have taken up during the autumn and which now makes them almost indistinguishable from their snowy background. And a further six months on will see them back in their summer suitings once again.

This ability to change colour in order to escape predators is not limited to seasonal changes. Many fish, for instance, change colour to 'match' the environment through

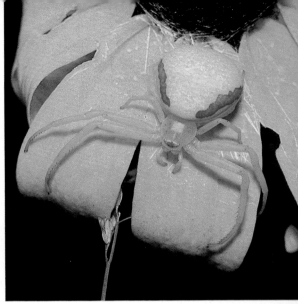

which they are moving. Its effectiveness has been demonstrated by putting fish into one kind of environment, taking them to another, and then letting loose predators among them. Up to twice as many get snapped up when their colour-change process has not had time to work.

In some cases this change takes place slowly, sometimes rapidly, but the mechanism is usually the same. The fish sees its surrounding environment and then, by means that are not fully understood even today, alters the arrangement of the pigment granules in its chromatophores or pigment cells. When these pigment granules are dispersed throughout each cell the fish is intensely coloured. However, if these granules become concentrated in the centre of each chromatophore the result is a lessening or disappearance of the predominant colour.

Some creatures, including birds and fishes, have evolved so that they are always camouflaged by 'counter-shading'; in other words their under parts, which in the case of birds will be in shadow when the birds are on the ground, are lighter than the upper portions of their bodies which will be in bright sunlight. The result is that they tend to merge into the landscape.

In addition to changes of colour, disruptive patterns also play an important part in the camouflage of some animals. This method, used by the armed forces in wartime when broken or wavy lines are used to conceal the outline of ships or planes, is well illustrated by the black and white butterfly fish whose curving bands of colour tend to make it unseen in the waters through which it swims. The mottled coats of some deer do the same job, making them almost indistinguishable from their normal background of bushes.

The process is carried to an extreme by the sargassum sea slug, one of the many creatures which live among seaweed. In this case not only the variegated colour but its shape helps it to fade into its background.

By contrast with these exotic examples, one of the most commonplace illustrations of everyday animal camouflage should not be forgotten: the pheasant whose mottled browns and greys make it almost invisible among moorland undergrowth until it flies up almost from one's feet.

(continued overleaf)

Opposite above: *The Varying hare in its winter fur, seen only with difficulty against the Alaskan snow and* (opposite below) *the nose-horned frog, almost invisible among dead leaves, so good is its camouflage.*

Top left and right: *The Crab-Spider in two different guises.*

Right: *Overleaf are examples of insects which resemble plants. Here mimicry is seen in a fly orchid, one of whose petals resembles an insect.*

(*continued from previous page*)

In the insect world there are many examples of 'camouflage' which go far beyond the colour-changes that the word normally suggests. Some of these more extreme forms were recorded more than a century ago by Henry Bates after his exploration of the Amazon – and after he had read Darwin's *Origin of Species* which helped to explain, among many other things, why some animals survive and others do not.

Insects often managed to escape their predators, Bates discovered, by resembling flowers, leaves, or other specific items in their environment. At times this process of survival by adaptation goes to extra-ordinary lengths. Thus the Indian leaf-bug is not only the shape and colour of the leaves among which it lives, but often clings to a twig and allows its body to swing back and forth like a leaf swaying in the wind. The Kallyma inachis butterfly of Assam shows bright orange and blue when it rests with open wings on a branch; but on the approach of an enemy it folds the wings and shows only their undersides – which are not only grained like the leaves of the local trees but even show white spots representing the mould that grows on them.

In Britain the scarce green and grey Merveille du Jour moth can be in-distinguishable from the patch of lichen on which it rests, while the broken colours of the Common Field Grasshopper make it difficult to detect from the grasses among which it lives. The grasshopper, *Truxalis grandis*, even has markings that resemble the veins of grass, and the grasshopper Oedipoda, although conspicuous in flight is quite a different thing when it comes in to land. As it closes its wings it apparently disappears. Treehoppers are not only coloured but also shaped so that when sucking juice from the stems of plants on which they feed they look like the sharp thorns usually avoided by predatory birds.

Stick insects in much the same way resemble the twigs on which they habitually rest; long thin creatures, they are difficult for even humans to distinguish from their surroundings. And 'looper' caterpillars also simulate small twigs. Some insects resemble not twigs but a whole stretch of bark – notably the European Pine Hawk Moth, a Flatid bug from Madagascar and an Indian bush-cricket.

The most extraordinary example of an insect looking like the plant or tree on which it is often found is the Peppered Moth. Until about 1850 this was only known as a light-coloured moth with faint grey markings. Then a black variety was found in Manchester. During the second half of the nineteenth century this black variety was found in continually larger numbers – but only in the industrial areas of Britain where the trees, leaves, and even walls had become blackened by smoke. Elsewhere the lighter variety was still found. In the 1920s, the British geneticist, J.B.S. Haldane, suggested that the Black Peppered Moth was the result of a genetic mutation and that those in the industrial areas had a 50 per cent better chance of survival than the lighter variety. Thirty years later, field studies proved him right.

Far left: *Many insects break their camouflage to adopt a defensive posture at the approach of an enemy. Here the Eyed Hawk moth is seen in its natural state (top) and giving a warning-off gesture (bottom) by displaying two 'eyes' on its wings.*

Left: *The Peppered Moth, self-camouflaged on tree-bark.*

Above right: *A looper caterpillar simulating a short twig; right: a leaf insect closely resembling the leaves on which it sits; and below: leaf hoppers looking like flowers on the stem of a plant.*

Chameleons

The Chameleons are among the most fascinating of all lizards. There are about 80 species, some less than five centimetres (2 in) long, others up to 0·6 metres (2 ft), but all possess a number of extraordinary features.

The best-known of these characteristics is their ability to change colour at will. A number of other lizards can do the same but the chameleon does so more quickly. The colour-change, in which the bright green turns to a pale yellow or dark brown, and the black spots of the animal disappear, is not entirely due to the colour of its surroundings; emotions also play their part.

It has been found that if a chameleon is blindfolded it will still change colour when the surrounding lights are changed. This shows that the mechanism of change, which operates through the layers of colour cells in the skin, is triggered off by light that falls on the skin rather than light which is seen by the eyes.

These eyes are among the chameleon's more remarkable features. Each is set in a hemispherical turret projecting from the animal's head and each can be swivelled independently of the other. It is therefore possible to see a chameleon with one eye looking up and one looking down; or with one looking forward while the other looks back.

It is a slow-mover and does not hunt its food. Instead, it waits silently until an insect moves into its range. First, one of the two eyes will see the prey; next, the second eye will swivel round so that the stereoscopic vision provided by the two of them together will give the distance. It is then that the most extraordinary feature of the chameleon is exhibited. Its mouth opens and out shoots a telescopic tongue that can be almost twice as long as the animal's body. The tip of the tongue, made adhesive with a special secretion in the animal's body, touches the insect and draws it back into the quickly-closing mouth. The whole operation is carried out in only one twenty-fifth of a second.

Chameleons have long coiled tails which they use when they move from branch to branch of the trees in which they live, and curiously-formed feet which end in two separate bundles of toes and give a firm hold on slippery boughs. Some species

The Mediterranean chameleon. Like other chameleon species, it changes colour at will, can swivel its two eyes independently of each other, and has a telescopic tongue.

have three ferocious-looking horns protruding from the head, but these are not, as might be thought, used in fighting. At the breeding season the chameleon may hiss and greatly distend its body, a practice which gave rise to the legend that it 'fed on air'. Most species lay eggs – up to as many as 40 – although a few give birth to living young. They are among the shortest-lived of reptiles and it is believed that few have a life of more than two years.

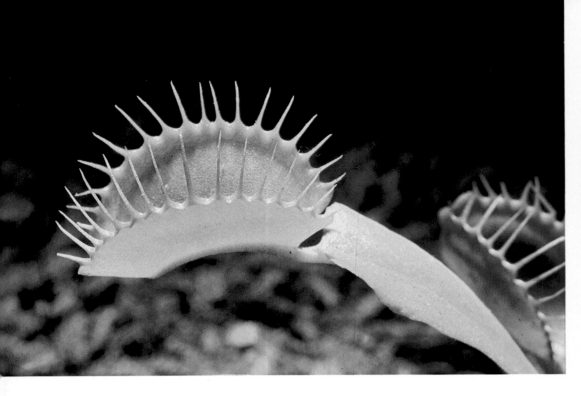

Carnivorous Plants

Plants that need 'meat' in their diet are remarkable enough in themselves. Even more strange is the variety of methods which they use to catch their prey.

Most insect-eating plants, of which there are at least 450 kinds, some found in many parts of the world, have one thing in common: they live in boggy areas where the soil is poor and where they have difficulty in obtaining the nitrogen essential to their life. Like other plants, they take in carbon dioxide through their leaves; but nitrogen is still necessary, and it is this that they obtain from the bodies of the insects which they catch, kill and digest.

The most famous of the carnivorous plants is probably the Venus Fly Trap, a brightly-coloured species which grows in the coastal swamps of North America and was thought by Charles Darwin to be the most wonderful plant in the world. It is a plant which catches its food by means of a 'snap trap', a form of leaf which ends in a hinged device an inch or so long. (See panel.)

Another trapping-method is used by the family of Bladderworts which feed on water insects. The tiny bladders operate by guiding an insect towards their mouth by tiny hairs. When the insect comes close enough, it touches one of these hairs near the plant's 'mouth'. The hairs act as triggers which open the door into the bladder. The insect is swept in with the rush of water that now fills the bladder, and the door then springs shut. Movement of the insect inside the bladder starts the release of liquids which dissolve the insect and allow the plant to make use of the nitrogen released.

Pitcher plants use a different method,

known as the pitfall trap. This involves encouraging an insect down the steepening internal slope of the pitcher-like leaves. Eventually the insect loses its foothold, is prevented from moving upwards by a series of downward-pointing hairs, and then drops into the liquid at the bottom of the pitcher where it is slowly digested. Since ants are very sure of their foothold but are a popular diet of some pitcher plants, these have evolved an ingenious mechanism which automatically shuts the entrance to the pitcher when the insect has progressed a certain way inside.

The extraordinary way in which plants can adapt themselves to different kinds of prey is shown by a fungus-carnivore which thrives in areas where the minute eel-worm is its favourite delicacy. The fungus sends out a narrow thread which curls up, over and down to form a tiny noose. When an eel-worm, wriggling along the ground, puts its head in the noose, this immediately tightens. Once the worm is dead, runners stretch out from the fungus to digest it.

Of all the methods which carnivorous plants use to catch their prey, one of the most simple is that of the fly-paper, used by the Sundew. Insects are attracted by the sticky fluid which is exuded from the stalked glands on the leaves. But the stickiness is more than they bargain for, and they cannot escape. Their struggles then act on the plant and cause it to release the digestive enzymes which destroy the insect's body.

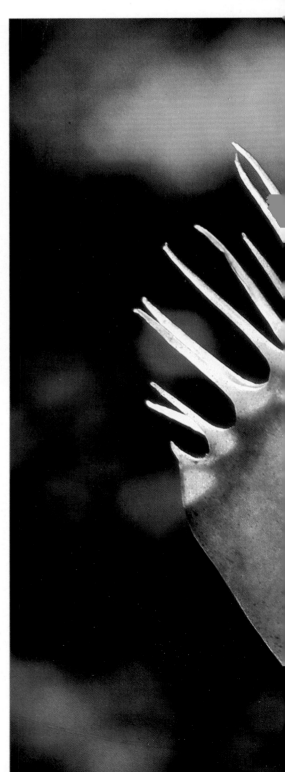

The Venus Fly Trap at work. A hungry plant awaits its prey (above left); *the fly alights* (above centre); *the plant's jaws snap shut* (above right). *The captive fly is still visible through the plant's semi-transparent skin* (right).

Migration and Navigation

Every year thousands of salmon leave the waters off Labrador or Greenland and start on a 2,000-mile journey that will bring them back to a river in Scotland: not any river but the very one in which they were spawned a few years previously. And every year thousands of birds make similar journeys – like the puffin which was taken across the Atlantic from its home in Wales, released in Boston, Mass., and was found 12 days later back in its hole on a Welsh cliffside. These are only two examples of the migration and navigation which takes place annually among mammals, fishes and birds and which after almost a century of scientific investigation is still only partially understood.

Many animal migrations, such as those of reindeer and the Arctic fox which move south at the beginning of the winter and return north at the beginning of the summer, are due to regular changes of climate. The same is true of the Alaskan fur seal which lives and breeds in the Bering

Sea from May to November, then swims 3,000 miles south to the warmer climate of southern California for the winter.

Some fish migrations have the same cause. Not so the amazing life-cycle of the salmon which begins its existence in fresh river waters. After one or two years, the young smolts are ready for a spring journey downstream to the sea. Little is known in detail about their future, although from one to three years can be spent in the waters of the north Atlantic. Returning, the fish seek out their own river – finding it, according to one theory, by its individual smell.

Great as are the riddles of navigation posed by migratory salmon, the annual migration of many millions of birds raises even greater ones. In Britain, the best-known example is provided by the swallows who every September set out on their many thousand mile flight to South Africa where they will winter before returning in April. The Arctic Tern breeds in the Yukon but migrates every year some 7,000 miles to Argentina; while swifts, which nest in Canada, winter on the borders of Antarctica before repeating their 12,000-mile flight in reverse the following spring.

The hard facts of bird-migration only began to be known about the turn of the century when the practice of ringing –

attaching a harmless identity tag to the bird's leg – was started. Within the last 30 years radar-tracking of migratory flights, and even the use of aircraft to follow birds, has produced many more facts. One bird, for instance, is known to have lived 27 years and flown half a million miles on its migratory flights.

Birds are known to 'feed up' before their migrations, and many weigh 30 per cent more than their normal weight before they set off. An increasing scarcity of insect-food as the time for migration approaches, variations in temperature, and even the changing length of daylight are among the factors which have been claimed as responsible for migration; but although these do vary considerably from year to year, migration dates change very little.

With bird migration, however, the 'how' is even more mysterious than the 'why'. During the last half-century scores of experiments have failed to show conclusively how birds navigate themselves halfway round the world with little apparent difficulty. It has been claimed that they have a means of utilizing magnetic forces. More plausibly, it has been claimed that they can navigate by sun or stars – and there have been many instances of migratory flights being interrupted when both

sun and stars have been obscured. Experiments in planetariums, where 'day' and 'night' can be artificially changed, tend to support the theory, but few clues have yet been discovered suggesting how birds do the trick.

Opposite above: *Massed Snow and Blue Geese landing on a lake in Dakota;* opposite below: *migration of reindeer and,* below, *wildebeeste.*

Above: *Hibernation is another animal survival technique; this is the common dormouse.*

Socially Organized Insects

One of the things which makes human beings different from other mammals is their social organization, their ability to divide up the jobs to be done in life so that some members co-operate in building, others produce or gather food and others have the task of defending the whole group. Yet the same division of labour is shown by several species in two orders of insects – the Hymenoptera and the Isoptera – whose members live together in colonies and carry out only one kind of work. Ants and bees are the best-known examples, but some wasps and all termites also live lives that in some ways almost uncannily resemble those of the human race.

There are no less than 5,000 species of ant but all of them are to greater or lesser degree organized in a social order, which is based on the three forms of each species. There are the queens, one to each colony, whose eggs provide new generations; there are short-lived males who die after a nuptial flight with the queen; and there are the worker ants, by far the most numerous, most of whom are female, though rarely sexual, and who show different forms according to the work they do. It is the worker ants who take the queen's eggs to the part of the colony where heat and humidity are best, and worker-nurses who care for the young ants. There are soldier-ants whose heads are bigger than normal, and harvester-ants whose task it is to find food and bring it back.

Some of the harvesters act as 'scouts'. After finding food in any quantity they carry samples back to the colony and while travelling produce from their body small drops of a special chemical substance to lead other harvesters to the food.

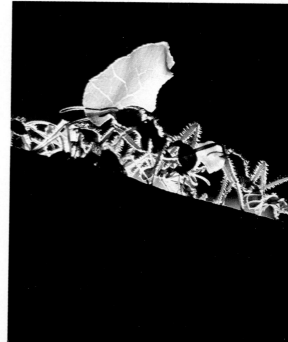

Among the bees, it is the honeybees and the bumblebees who are socially organized. In the case of both species, the queen, ruling over a hive of up to 60,000 bees, can lay between 1,000 and 2,000 eggs a day. These are cared for by the workers until the infant bees emerge from the pupae. They spend the first three or four days cleaning their surroundings, then start feeding the bees who have hatched out a few days earlier. At the age of two weeks the young bees will start producing beeswax from special glands in their bodies, and also comb-building. Only at the age of about three weeks will they start the job on which they will spend the next three to five weeks that will complete their life span – foraging for nectar, pollen and water.

The fate of the queens' fertilized larvae depends on their diet. Those given only honey and pollen develop into workers. Some are given protein-rich food produced by glands in the mouths of the workers and known as 'royal jelly'; as a result they grow into queens.

For long it was not known how a worker bee who found a good supply of food while foraging was able to direct other members of the hive to it. The extraordinary method, discovered by the Austrian entomologist von Frisch, involves a dance made by the returning bee. This first indicates whether the source is nearby or distant and then shows the direction in which it lies. To execute this complicated manoeuvre the bee must know the position of the sun, and scientists were at first puzzled by the fact that the food-location could be successfully given even on dull days. The answer, they found, was that the bee can detect the sun's position by the pattern of polarized light in the sky.

Insect organization: a termite heap in Senegal (opposite above); ants foraging on a leaf (opposite below) and carrying it home (below); bees in a swarm (right) and a queen bee inspecting cells (below right).

The Spider's Web

The spider's web, immensely strong for its weight, is one of the wonders of the insect world – and one of the most beautiful. But the silk of which the web is made is very much more than that for the spider – it is the means by which she protects her eggs and young, catches food, orientates herself to her surroundings, and even crosses patches of water after the silk has been specially ballooned up.

The most familiar spider's web is the 'orb web', produced by about 40 of the world's 40,000 species. The silk of which it is constructed is a viscous sticky fluid produced by glands in the spider's abdomen. This fluid comes from the spider's body by one or more of six spinnerets which contain a total of between 60 and 70 outlets. The silk cannot, however, be forced out of the spider's body; it must be drawn out. Sometimes this is done by the wind, which can blow a small drop of thread into a long line. Sometimes the manoeuvre is accomplished entirely by the spider which

will press its spinneret on to the ground, fix the drop of exposed silk to the ground in doing so, and then walk away. As the line of silk is produced, the stretching which takes place reorientates the fibrous constituents of the silk and in doing so hardens it. The faster the silk is drawn out the stronger it will be.

This variation of speed is not the only way in which the spider can control the details of the web it builds. These will also be governed by the site, the strength and direction of the wind and even, it is sometimes claimed, by the abundance of edible insects in the neighbourhood.

Whatever the minor differences, the spider will always build its web by the same succession of actions. First will come the 'bridge thread' on which the rest of the web will depend; sometimes this will be formed by the spider swinging across from a thread whose end it has attached to a leaf or a twig; sometimes it will be the result of a wind-blown thread fortuitously attaching itself. Next, the spider travels along this first thread, reinforcing it as it goes, before forming a multi-sided outer framework of threads. With the framework intact, the spider then spins a number of internal

Above: *The beautiful detail of a spider's web.*

threads, each going from a 'leg' of the outer framework and crossing each other at what will be the centre of the finished web.

Now, starting at the point where the threads all cross, the spider makes a spiral course outwards from the centre to the circumference of the web. Having reached this after numerous circuits, and after having laid down what is a form of spiral 'scaffolding', the spider retraces the route. At intervals she will stretch the coated line before releasing it with a jerk so that minute beads of the sticky material are formed along the thread. Finally, a signal thread is laid from the centre of what is now a lair as well as a web. This will be set moving as soon as an insect gets caught in the web.

Quite apart from acting as a trap for the insects which form the spider's diet, the silken strands are used to help form cocoons for eggs. In the autumn they can often be seen as long lines of thin silk gossamer. These, if taken up by the wind, can be numerous enough and strong enough to make a spider airborne.

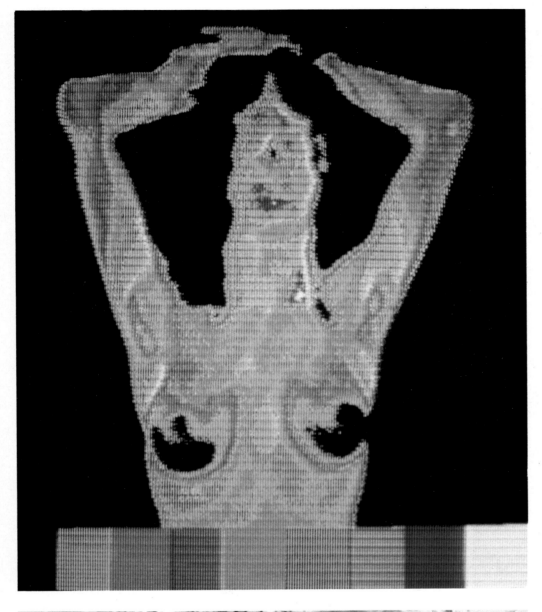

The Human Body

The greatest wonder of all has attracted the attention it deserves only with the advance of science during the last few decades. It is the human body with its 50,000,000,000,000 (50 million million) cells, with a brain containing 10,000,000,000 (ten thousand million) special cells called neurons, and with a vastly complicated mechanism which enables it to maintain life in the most discouraging circumstances.

Man has been interested in his body since he first climbed down out of the trees, but he has begun to know the details only as doctors and medical scientists have unravelled how the body works. The huge numbers of cells have different tasks in this complicated operation. There are the food-absorbing cells, which line the intestine and absorb the post-digested food into the bloodstream; the red and white blood cells, the first distributing oxygen from the lungs to the rest of the body and the white cells helping to destroy microbes; the reproductive cells; and the muscle cells, very long cells whose task it is to produce movement.

This movement takes place when the muscles receive the necessary signals. These signals are sent to them along one of the signal-carrying networks that are among the most recently understood marvels of the human body. The networks, or nerves consist of neurons, or nerve-cells, and are actuated by the cortex of the brain which itself contains some ten thousand million neurons. The cortex is a sheet of material only one or two millimetres thick. If spread out, it would cover between 1,500 and 2,200 square centimetres (232–341 sq in) but it is, instead, deeply folded up into two hemispheres. Different parts of these hemispheres are, in effect, the control areas for different signal-networks. One area receives signals from receptors in the sense organs, another deals with decision-making, while a third makes use of a network which instructs the muscles what to do.

The brain, and the central nervous system with which it works, are delicate and are therefore protected by a shock-absorbing fluid and the bones of the skull and the spine. Other bones protect vulnerable parts of the body, the ribs, for instance, providing a protective cage for the heart and the lungs.

Above: *A thermogram of the human body.*

Below: *A hugely magnified portion of human skin showing, in foreground, a single human hair.*

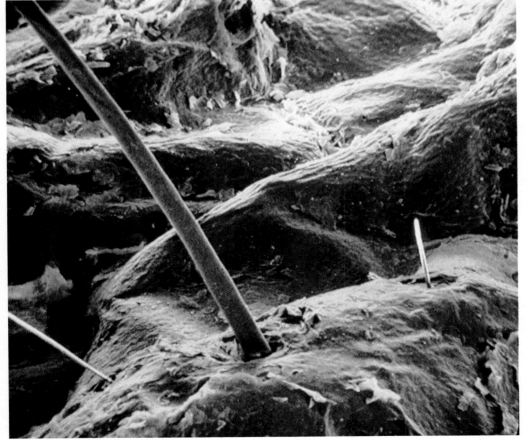

MAN-MADE WONDERS

Machu Picchu

On 24 July 1911 Hiram Bingham, a young American explorer, was led by a native guide across the foaming waters of the Peruvian river Urubamba, up 600 metres (2,000 ft) of precipitous snake-infested slopes, to the solitary hut of two farmers who had successfully hacked a patch of agricultural land from the surrounding undergrowth. Here, 2,330 metres (7,650 ft) above sea level, on a narrow neck of land almost surrounded by a U-bend of the river, there was at first little to be seen. Then, rounding a promontory, Bingham met 'an unexpected sight, a great flight of beautifully-constructed stone-faced terraces, perhaps a hundred of them, each hundreds of feet long and 10 feet high. . . . Suddenly I found myself confronted with the walls of ruined houses built of the finest quality Inca stone-work. It was hard to see them for they were partly covered with trees and moss, the growth of centuries, but in the dense shadow, hiding in bamboo thickets and tangled vines, appeared here and there walls of white granite ashlars carefully cut and exquisitely fitted together.'

Bingham had discovered Machu Picchu, the lost city of the Incas, unknown even to the Spanish conquerors of the sixteenth century and abandoned for more than 300 years.

The ruined city, unique in its isolation, dominated by the 150-metre (500-ft) peak of Huyana Picchu which rose at the end of the ridge, and overshadowed by the more distant peaks of the Andes, was more than a great discovery. 'In the sublimity of its surroundings, the marvel of its site, the character and the mystery of its construction', it has been said, 'the Western Hemisphere holds nothing comparable.'

Bingham took such details of the extraordinary site as he had time for and returned to the United States. There he persuaded Yale University and the National Geographic Society to finance expeditions which would scientifically explore the site. He returned to lead the work first in 1911, then in 1915. The excavation of what had been one of the most important cities of the Inca Empire provided much new information on how men and women had lived during one of the great periods of South American civilization. A 'welfare state', run under the control of the divine 'Inca' or emperor, the Inca Empire was supported by a religion based on worship of the Sun. The most remarkable features of Machu Picchu are the buildings themselves: houses, temples and shrines built of white granite and consisting of blocks hewn with extraordinary accuracy in view of the primitive tools used, and then fitted together without the use of masonry.

At the time of its discovery, Machu Picchu could be reached only after a three-day journey, by mule and on foot, from the city of Cuzco, 50 miles away and a town of 200,000 inhabitants when Machu Picchu was at the height of its prosperity. Today the site has become a great tourist attraction and can be reached by train and by car in a day.

Above: *An aerial view showing the road leading to the ruins and* (opposite) *the ruins as they have now been restored.*

Previous pages: *The space-shuttle.*

53

Chichen-Itza

Surrounded by the encroaching Mexican jungle, the highly sculptured temples of Chichen-Itza today form one of the most spectacular examples of a great civilization that rose and fell within a few hundred years.

The first city of the name was founded early in the sixth century in the inhospitable limestone country of north Yucatan, some 50 miles from the Gulf of Mexico. Water is scarce throughout the whole area except where the ground has subsided to reveal underground watercourses, and two such *cenotes*, close together, encouraged the first Mayas to settle at what was to become a famous site. In fact the name of the city came from the Mayan word for mouth, 'chi'; the word 'chen' meaning 'water-well'; and the name of the Itza tribe.

The first Chichen-Itza was abandoned after less than 200 years, without achieving much importance. It was reoccupied at the start of the tenth century; but another 200 years passed before the conquest of the Itzans by other Mayan tribes led to a sudden growth of the city, the building of monuments and temples whose ruins still inspire awe, and the creation of a savage civilization.

Human sacrifices were regularly made by hurling victims into one of the deep *cenotes*. This was the end of a journey which began a quarter of a mile away on the 30-metre (100-ft) Castillo, the great Temple of Kukulcan, 'the Feathered Serpent'. The Castillo is a four-sided pyramid, covering an acre (0·4 hectares) and rising in nine receding terraces, these being traver-sed on each of the four sides by stone stairways. From the top of the Castillo one looks down on to the quarter-mile Via Sacra which leads to the Cenote of Sacrifice.

Even more impressive than the Castillo is the Group of the 1,000 Columns, an 11-hectare (27-acre) complex of temples, halls, courts and terraces whose hundreds of stone columns, square and round, plain and sculptured, indicate the magnificence of Chichen-Itza in its heyday. The inhabitants appear to have had considerable mathematical knowledge and remains still exist of the astronomical observatory, a tower 23-metres (75-ft) high, housing two circular corridors with doors at the four cardinal points of the compass through which observations could be made.

In 1923 the Carnegie Institution of Washington began a 10-year campaign of excavations at Chichen-Itza. The problems faced by the archaeologists are underlined by one of their reports on a 28 × 3 metre (93 × 11 ft) mammoth mosaic of cut stone which they discovered in one of the temples: 'The wreck, scores upon scores of intricately sculptured blocks strewing the terrace in front – feathers, shields, jaguars, macaws, elements of the famous mayan mask panels, human figures, snake heads, snake tails and bodies scattered about in indescribable confusion – have constituted for the investigators, in their attempts to assemble them, a veritable giant's jig-saw puzzle, the individual pieces of which are heavy blocks of stone.'

Left: *Part of the Group of 1,000 columns.*
Above: *The Castillo.*

Shwe Dagon Pagoda

With its gold-encrusted summit rising 113 metres (370 ft) above the surrounding countryside, the Shwe Dagon Pagoda outside Rangoon in Burma is the most revered and most ancient shrine in the whole of Indo-China. Its attraction for the pilgrims who visit it from all parts of the Far East is that it contains relics of all the four Buddhas who have so far appeared: Kaukathan's 'Drinking Cup', Gaunagohn's 'Robe'; Kathapa's 'Staff'; and the 'Eight Hairs' of Gautama.

The word pagoda comes from a Persian phrase meaning 'idol-temple' and usually refers to a building resembling a pyramid in shape. In Burma, the land of pagodas, there are three kinds: the masonry temples, the carved and ornamental wooden buildings which include wooden shrines and even rest-houses, and the pagodas enshrining relics, such as the Shwe Dagon which stands on a rectangular terrace cut into a hillside between the Hlaing and Pegu rivers.

It was here that eight hairs of Gautama were brought in a gold casket and added to 'a water dipper, a bathing garment, and a staff' owned by his predecessors. An 8-metre (27-ft) pagoda was built over the relics, and religious buildings sprang up nearby. Yet nearly 2,000 years passed before the local ruler, Binya-Ran, decided to enlarge the shrine. His successors carried on the work, raising the height first to 40 metres (130 ft) then to 98 metres (320 ft) and setting apart land for more buildings as well as slaves for their upkeep.

In 1774 the reigning king, Shin-byu-shin, re-gilded the structure with his own weight in gold, 77·6 kg (171 lb). A further re-gilding took place in 1834, and in 1871 the reigning king, Mindon Min, added the massive *hti*, or umbrella, which forms the top of the pagoda today. This umbrella consists of a number of circular iron rings which decrease in size towards the top, where the gem crown is fixed. All the iron hoops are covered with beaten gold and from them there hang scores of gold and silver bells which keep up a constant sound as they are moved by the wind.

The pagoda is approached by a covered stairway from the south where there congregate beggars, lepers, and stall-keepers who live by selling candles, flags, and other offerings for the worshippers. Above, there is a flagged courtyard surrounded by shrines and other buildings while above this again there rise the tapering surfaces of the pagoda with its tinkling bells.

The Shwe Dagon Pagoda is famous not only for its religious sanctity and the extraordinary form of its tapering pinnacle but also for the huge 43-ton bell housed in a separate building on the eastern side of the raised platform on which the complex of buildings stands. Standing 4 metres (14 ft) high and made of metal 38 cm (15 in) thick, the bell is one of the largest in the Far East.

Opposite: *The lesser shrines and guardian beasts surrounding Shwe Dagon.*

Left: *The extraordinary tapering pinnacle of the Shwe Dagon pagoda.*

Angkor Wat

Deep in Cambodia, and kept free from the inroads of the surrounding jungle only by the constant efforts of Buddhist monks, lies the huge religious complex of Angkor Wat, nearly a square mile of temples, towers and terraces. One temple alone contains more than 1,500 columns, all hewn from a site more than 30 miles away and testimony to the immense labours needed for the building of what King Suryavarman II hoped would be his funeral monument.

The fantastic architecture of Angkor Wat followed that of earlier pyramid-temples, but in size, scope and decoration it was far more ambitious. The history of Angkor itself goes back to the eighth century but it was only after 1113, when

Suryavarman II overcame his enemies in a one-day battle, that work was begun on the great complex of sandstone buildings. From the west they are approached across a bridge spanning an encircling moat. Beyond this there rises a three-tiered outer wall two-and-a-half miles long and more than 182 metres (600 ft) wide, and beyond this again there stretches a quarter-mile-long, nine-metre (30 ft) wide paved highway leading to the central temple-enclosure on which thousands of men laboured for the 25 years between 1125 and 1150.

Lined with ornate balustrades which are decorated with complicated sculptures of seven-headed snakes, the stone highway leads across a great lake towards the central temple enclosure from which the five great towers of the main temple complex can be seen rising towards the sky. These five towers represent the five peaks of Mount Meru, the fabulous mountain of Hindu mythology, 80,000 leagues high and lying at the centre of the earth. Surrounding it, the walls and the waters represent the earth and the oceans.

If the buff, ochre, and pink sandstone of which the Angkor temples are built makes them among the most colourful buildings of the east, they have two other remarkable features. One is the craftsmanship which gives the buildings the air of having been carved out of the living rock. No sign of mortar, no mark of chisel, reveals how the work was done and the walls, stairways and balustrades appear to have grown out of the country rather than to have been built on it.

The second and most remarkable feature of Angkor Wat, however, is the carvings that cover almost every available square foot of wall, tower, balustrade or ceiling. Mythical beasts, the tevodas or celestial women who inhabit heaven; scenes from early Cambodian history, gods, goddesses and godlings, and stories from the Ramayana (an epic Sanskrit poem) all appear in flourishing and exotic detail. The humid atmosphere of Cambodia has over the centuries taken the early freshness from these extraordinary scenes of what happened long ago. Yet the work of French archaeologists during the first third of this century has succeeded in preserving a great deal – so that Angkor Wat is today still one of the wonders of the east.

Opposite above: *Some of the elaborate ruins of Angkor Wat.*

Opposite below: *The main temple.*

Above: *Ta Keo, one of the numerous other temples on the site.*

The Great Wall of China

Once called the Eighth Wonder of the World, the Great Wall of China stretches for more than a thousand miles from the Gulf of Chihli on the Yellow Sea to the frontiers of Tibet. The greatest single building operation ever carried out by man, it has been claimed to be the only sign of human activity that would be visible from Mars.

Although stretches of the Great Wall have been reconstructed throughout the centuries, it is the achievement of Ch'in Shih Huang Ti, the country's first Emperor from whose first name comes the 'China' we use today. Small stretches of fortification had been built from the earliest times in the areas where the comparatively fertile country of China changes into the wastes of the Gobi Desert and the other barren areas to the north. In 220 BC, however, Ch'in Shih Huang Ti had the grandiose idea of building a major new defence work which would link these short stretches, reinforce them, and provide an impregnable barrier against invasion from the north.

From the first defence tower, on the seacoast at Shanhaikwan, the Wall runs westwards to end on the top of a precipice some 1,525 metres (5,000 ft) high overlooking the Great North River. In a straight line the distance is 1,145 miles. But the Wall, twisting and turning to follow the best line of the country, is estimated to be about 1,700 miles long – the distance from London to Leningrad or from New York to Denver. Even this, however, is not a complete indication of the builders' extraordinary achievement since at places sidewalls run off from the main line, then double back on themselves to reinforce the defences, an addition that brings the actual length of the structure to about 2,500 miles.

Sometimes six metres (20 ft) high, sometimes nine metres (30 ft), the Wall was built on a sloping granite foundation which at its top is wide enough to take four or five horsemen abreast. This top pavement was flanked by a 1·5-metre (5-ft) high parapet, crenellated to give protection to bowmen.

While the core of the Wall was heavily-tamped earth, this was – with the exception of a few western sections – finished with carefully cut stone, or bricks. In all, it has been estimated that about 11,960 cubic metres (422,400 cu ft) of material was needed for every mile.

The Wall was further reinforced by thousands of defence towers. These were sited 8 or 12 to the mile according to the lie of the land, the theory being that all approaches to the northern side of the wall would be within bow-shot. In addition, the defences were strengthened by isolated watch-towers, built on commanding heights within a mile or so of the wall. The aim of their garrisons was to give the Wall's defenders warning of enemy forces, and each watch-tower was stocked with food, water, fuel and weapons for a four-month siege.

Estimates of the time taken to build the Wall, and the number of men involved, can only be rough but it has been suggested that up to a million labourers, troops, prisoners-of-war and slaves were at work for some of the 20 or more years that the job took. Many men died as the work progressed. So many were buried under the Wall itself that it has been called the longest cemetery in the world.

Although it was once claimed by General Meng Tien, in charge of the original construction, that only nine men were needed to garrison each mile of the wall, large forces were usually stationed in the 'back areas'. They, like the Wall, failed to be effective and the 2,000 years after its construction have seen many invasions. In many places there has been re-building over the centuries and in some western stretches the Wall has deteriorated badly. At the Nankow Pass it is now traversed by the Pekin-Kalgan railway, and the eastern stretches are a tourist attraction. Yet for hundreds of miles its sinuous course, winding across peaks and through valleys, is still an astonishing tribute to the men who planned and built it.

The Great Wall of China threading its way across country and (below) a close-up of the eastern portion of the wall near Peking.

The Acropolis

Although the word 'acropolis' means the highest part, or citadel, of a Greek city, there is only one part of the world that is known as 'the Acropolis'. This is the craggy rock in the city of Athens, rising some 150 metres (500 ft) above the surrounding areas and crowned with the remains of ancient Greek buildings, notably the Parthenon, that are world-famous as the finest of their kind.

There had been buildings on this naturally defendable position since prehistoric times, but it was only during the reign of Pericles in the fifth century BC that the Parthenon was built – between 447 and 432 BC – as a temple to the goddess Athena Parthenos. The huge temple, more than 30 metres (100 ft) wide and nearly 70 metres (230 ft) long and the world's finest example of the Doric style of architecture, remained virtually undamaged for almost a thousand years. Other temples were built on the Acropolis, notably the Erechtheum, built in the Ionic style but with features not known elsewhere.

In the seventh century AD the Parthenon was turned into a Christian church and, after the capture of Athens by the Turks in 1458, into a mosque. It was still intact when, in 1687, a shot from a Venetian ship bombarding Athens hit a powder store in the cellars. The explosion which followed caused great damage. Then, at the start of the nineteenth century, the seventh Earl of Elgin, British Ambassador to Greece, had the unique frieze from the Parthenon removed and brought to Britain. It is known as the Elgin Marbles, housed in the British Museum, and shows the great Athenian festival, the Panathenaic procession to the Acropolis which culminates with the investiture of Athena in a sacred violet robe.

Today the Parthenon, the temple of Athena Nike, the Erechtheum, and many of the other buildings on the Acropolis have been carefully restored. Most of the statues, frescoes, and ornaments which once made the buildings of the Acropolis a unique wonder of the world have gone, some taken by the Romans, others destroyed and yet others removed by the succession of Italians, Venetians, Arabs and other invaders over the centuries. Despite this, the remains of the Parthenon with its sublime Doric pillars still provides the visitor with an unequalled example of ancient Greek architecture at the pinnacle of its development.

In the summer the site is rich in wildflowers. On the summit of the Acropolis they grow up between the marble slabs while many can be seen on the steep cliff-faces where the yellow flowers of the Prickly Pear, a cactus introduced in the sixteenth century, flourishes from May onwards.

Right: *An aerial view of the Acropolis showing the Parthenon* (below) *in the centre of the site.*

Stonehenge

Mystery still surrounds the exact origin and purpose of Stonehenge, the prehistoric monument on Salisbury Plain, some 10 miles north of Salisbury, Wiltshire. The group of standing stones, arranged in concentric circles and the greatest of its kind in Europe, was for long thought to have been mainly a place of worship. The stone circles have also been described as an astronomical temple from which the length of the year would be found by watching the place of the sunrise on the longest day. It is possible that the two functions were combined, but considerable doubt remains.

If the reasons for building Stonehenge are still obscure, the excavations of the twentieth century have produced much hard evidence of when and how the stones were erected. There appear to have been three main construction periods, the first of which, dated to about 1800 BC, has no connection with the vertical stones and their horizontal capstones which provide the familiar picture of Stonehenge. During this first stage a circular bank about 97 metres (320 ft) across was raised on the flat surface of the chalk downs, with an 'entrance' left on the north-east side. Inside this circular bank there was a ring of 56 pits, today known as Aubrey holes after John Aubrey who discovered them in the seventeenth century – and who originated the idea that Stonehenge was connected with the Druids.

A huge 35-ton horizontal block of local sandstone known as the Heel stone, outside the entrance to the bank, is believed to have belonged to this initial building phase, but the first standing stones arrived a century or more later. These were the famous 'bluestones', found only in the Prescelly Mountains of South Wales, on the far side of the Bristol Channel and about 140 miles in a straight line from Stonehenge. The riddle of how the bluestones could have been moved this distance by prehistoric people was solved some years ago when 'mock' stones of the same size and weight were moved on rollers from the Prescelly Mountains to the Bristol Channel, floated on supports up the Channel to the Wiltshire Avon, then up the Avon to a point where they were again moved overland – all with the use only of simulated prehistoric materials. These bluestones were set up in the form of two concentric circles; but they were later demolished and it was only in the third stage, believed to have been about another century later, that today's picture of Stonehenge began to emerge.

During this final stage some 80 large

blocks of sarsen, the sandstone boulders found on the Marlborough Downs some 20 miles to the north, were brought to Stonehenge, presumably by methods similar to those used for the bluestones. These huge sarsens, up to 50 tons in weight, were then erected in two arrangements, one being a circle of uprights capped by a continuous stone lintel, the other being a horseshoe inside the circle.

There are three remarkable features of the sarsens, which were hewn into shape with stone hammers. One is that the horizontal slabs forming the lintel are curved lengthwise to fit the circle. In addition they have been cut broader at the top than at the bottom, thus compensating for foreshortening when seen from the ground. Thirdly, the stones have hollowed-out mortices which fit on to tenons carved to jut out from the tops of the uprights – a remarkable achievement for people using primitive tools.

To complete the third stage, the dismantled bluestones were re-erected in a circle and a horseshoe to make the four-fold structure whose remains can be seen

Left: *The prehistoric stone circles of Stonehenge.*

Right: *John Constable's powerful painting of the monument, carried out in 1835.*

today. In the centre of the monument is the Altar Stone, a sandstone block from South Wales, apparently erected first as a pillar and later falling to its present horizontal position.

While the uses to which Stonehenge was put are still under dispute, it is clear that it was a central meeting point in prehistoric times. Salisbury Plain was – and still is – a central plateau of chalk from which chalk ridges radiate in all directions. These comparatively open chalk ridges formed the great highways of prehistory and the Plain, as well as the ridges running from it, are scattered thickly with the barrows, tumuli and other memorials of the men and women who lived up to 4,000 years ago.

Easter Island

More than two-and-a-half centuries ago Admiral Jacob Roggeveen, captain of the Dutch ship *Arena*, dropped anchor off a minute speck of land in the Pacific. The year was 1722, the date Easter Sunday. The island, of about 46 square miles – roughly the size of Jersey – lay some 2,300 miles from the coast of Chile to the east, and about the same distance from Tahiti to the west. The nearest land was the small dot in the ocean known as Pitcairn Island, more than 1,000 miles away.

When the crew of the *Arena* went ashore on what their captain had christened Easter Island, they saw, standing on long stone platforms around the coast, dozens of extraordinary stone figures. These statues, 'thin-lipped, disdainful of aspect and capped by crowns of red tufa' as they have been described, were as much as six metres (20 ft) high. They all appeared to have an almost 'family' resemblance, and the Dutchmen found it difficult to understand how the huge figures, obviously weighing many tons, could have been carved and then dragged into position by the natives. Since that day in 1722 the Easter Island statues have been a constant source of mystery to all who have visited the island – explorers, archaeologists and anthropologists.

Fifty years after Admiral Roggeveen's discovery, Spain formally annexed Easter Island. In 1774 Captain Cook visited the island, and gave the first lengthy description of the extraordinary statues. Halfway through the nineteenth century the Chileans, needing labour for the newly-exploited guano deposits along their coast, raided Easter Island and carried away 1,000 of the inhabitants. Only a handful of the islanders returned – bringing with them the smallpox germs which quickly devastated the families they rejoined. Throughout the present century Easter Island has been the goal of a long line of investigators. One of the most recent was Thor Heyerdahl, who in 1956–7 scientifically excavated many of the statues and gave at least partial answers to the questions they raised.

Easter Island appears to have been colonized during the fourteenth century by Polynesians sailing or paddling from the west. Some 300 years later a second flood of immigrants led to bitter fighting between what have traditionally been known as the 'long ears' and the 'short ears'. Heyerdahl discovered that the site where the 'long ears' are reputed to have died was in fact a defensive site whose ditch was filled with ashes.

The statues were carved from a soft stone consisting of compressed volcanic ash found on the north-east of the island. Although each was many tons in weight – but much less than the reputed 100 tons – they were then hauled with the help of ropes and rollers to the platforms or *aku* and slowly raised into position. These *aku* were funerary platforms on which the dead were exposed before being moved to stone vaults below. Up to 15 statues have been found on a single platform of which about 250 are still in existence.

Despite the fact that tentative answers have now been given to the riddles of Easter Island, much still remains unknown. As Heyerdahl himself has written: 'The air is laden with mystery; bent on you is the silent gaze of a hundred and fifty eyeless faces. The huge standing figures look down at you with an enigmatic stare; your steps are watched from every single ledge and cave in the mountain, where giants unborn and giants dead and broken lie as in mangers and on sick-beds, lifeless and helpless because the intelligent creative force has left them.'

Above: *Five of Easter Island's impressive and mysterious statues.*

The Pyramids

One of the most impressive buildings ever constructed, the Great Pyramid of Gizeh, standing in the desert a few miles south-west of Cairo, consists of some 2,300,000 two-and-a-half-ton blocks of stone, laid so accurately that the 232-metre (760-ft) base-lines are no more than seven inches out of true. And the four corners of the pyramid, oriented towards the four cardinal points of the compass, are only one-tenth of a degree out of true.

Rising to a height of about 139 metres (455 ft), the Great Pyramid was built about 3,700 BC and legend maintains that the task took 100,000 men more than 20 years. While these figures are now discounted, the building was certainly a massive task, its aim being to provide a funeral monument for King Khufu. Two other pyramids nearby provide tombs for other reigning monarchs of the fourth dynasty, while throughout Egypt nearly 80 other pyramids have been recorded, smaller in size but basically of the same design. For years it was believed that the huge quadrangular erections, rising in massive stone steps, had some astronomical or prophetic significance and complicated theories were worked out from measurement of the sides and slopes of the pyramids. The great British archaeologist Flinders Petrie once met a man measuring the side of one long step with a tape and a chisel. The chisel, he was told, was to 'adjust' the length of the side to accord with a theory!

It is known today that the pyramids were built solely as elaborate last resting places for the ruling pharaohs who planned them from the time they came to power. Little is known with certainty about the methods used for building, but it is believed that the stone slabs were hewn close to the pyramid-sites – and then hauled on sleds. The granite used for lining the interior sepulchres, or burial vaults, of the pyramids was floated down the Nile from quarries near Aswan and then hauled into position.

The first sepulchral chamber of the Great Pyramid of Gizeh was hewn out of the solid rock beneath the pyramid, and reached by a 98-metre (320-ft) passage from an entrance which descended to it from an entrance at the foot of the pyramid. Next, a second chamber, reached by an ascending passage, was built deep within the pyramid. This also was superceded and a third chamber was then built in the centre of the pyramid. This was reached by an extension passage from the second chamber and lay directly below the top of the pyramid. The interiors of all three chambers were faced with granite, and specially fine limestone was also used for capping the exterior of the whole erection. Much of this has been taken during the last few thousand years and used for the building of mosques and houses in Cairo.

Right: The Great Pyramid of Gizeh, built by Pharaoh Cheops, flanked by the lesser pyramids of Chephren and Mykerinos.

The Taj Mahal

It has been said to have 'a peculiar charm which distinguishes it from any other building in the world.' It has been described as 'within more measurable distance of perfection than any other work of man.' And few of those who pass through the blood-red sandstone walls surrounding the Taj Mahal disagree with these verdicts on the astonishing white marble of the mausoleum which rises in front of them.

More than three-and-a-half centuries ago the great Indian ruler Shah Jahan – 'the King of the World' – married a young Indian princess, Arjumand Bano Begam, soon known as Muntaz Mahal or 'the ornament of the palace'. Following their marriage in 1612, the wife bore the ruler eight sons and six daughters; then, in 1631, she died in childbirth. Her widower, already known for architectural and artistic extravagances which included the Peacock Throne later taken to Persia, decreed that a unique mausoleum should be built for his wife and himself on the banks of the Jumma River outside the great city of Agra.

First, plans were prepared by a committee of architects drawn from India, Persia, and the most distant parts of Asia. It is generally accepted that the prototype followed was the tomb of Humayun, built in Delhi, and there is little evidence for the often quoted claim that the architect was an Italian. A body of craftsmen was ordered to the task of carrying out the ambitious project. There were 22,000 of them in all, and their work was to take more than 20 years.

Inside the walls surrounding the building that now arose – named the Taj Mahal after a corruption of the words for 'the ornament of the palace' – stretch formal gardens with avenues of cypresses and long narrow lily-ponds. These lead to the mausoleum and two smaller buildings flanking it on either side. The mausoleum, almost 19 metres (200 ft) square, is of white marble, with a great arch cut into each side, standing 33 metres (108 ft) high and surmounted by a bulbous double dome which rises almost 76 metres (250 ft) above the surrounding grounds. Standing separate from each corner of the building there rises a three-storied 42-metre (138-ft) minaret.

If the exterior of the Taj Mahal is unique in its symmetrical beauty, the interior is unrivalled in the elaborate mosaic work and the details of the stone-studded perforated marble screens of the central octagonal chamber. Lapis lazuli, jasper, blood-stone, agates, cornelians and jade are among the stones which the inlayers used for decoration. The elaboration of the ornament can be judged by the fact that up to 100 stones have in some cases been used to produce a single flower.

The light goes into the central apartment through double screens of white marble trellis-work of immensely intricate design. One is on the outer and one on the inner face of the walls and in Britain this would result in almost complete darkness; but in India, where the light is far more glaring, and in a building of white marble, the double screens are necessary to temper what would otherwise be an intolerable glare.

Right: *The perfect symmetry of the exterior of the Taj Mahal.*

Below: *The marble screen which surrounds the central octagonal chamber.*

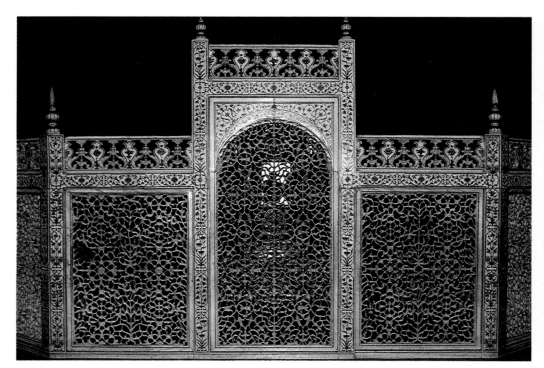

The Isfahan Mosques

Eighteen million bricks and half a million brightly coloured tiles used in a single building – that is a measure of the unique brilliance of the Isfahan mosques, no less than 162 of which once ornamented what, four centuries ago, was the capital of Persia. Today the city, which in the 1700s was larger than London, still contains a unique collection of buildings illustrating Moslem art at its richest and finest.

The 'Golden Age' of Isfahan, 1,525 metres (5,000 ft) above sea level and in the centre of what is now Iran, began in 1598 when Shah Abbas the Great moved his court to it from Kazvin, and continued until his death in 1629. Only 21 in 1598, the Shah determined to make the city the most beautiful of its day. He succeeded, by ambitious town-planning and the extensive use of the local craftsmen who were even then known for their skills in the making of faïence-mosaic and polychrome tiles.

The Shah's plans were centred on the Maidan, an eight-hectare (20-acre) open space bordered by a narrow canal of running water beyond which rise lines of doubly arcaded buildings. Some of these were the most beautiful buildings in the world. The greatest was the Royal Mosque on the south side of the Maidan, entered under a huge arch nearly 27 metres (90 ft) high, flanked by complexly ornamented turquoise-coloured walls which rise from marble pedestals. The Mosque itself, built round a great court and covered by a huge turquoise dome, was one of the most splendid examples of Islamic art in the world.

The glory of the Shah's Mosque was achieved despite his anxiety to have it finished as fast as possible. One of the architects was ordered to hurry on before the foundations had set properly and only saved the situation by going into hiding until he could prove that he was right. And to save time a new sort of tile that could be fired more quickly, but was less brilliant, was used for parts of the work. Even so, the great mosque was not finished until a few years after the Shah's death.

On the east side of the Maidan there rose the Shaikh Lutfullah Mosque, built in honour of the Shah's father-in-law and incorporating what is often claimed to be the richest decoration in all Isfahan. Facing it across the Maidan was the Ali Qapu 'gateway' leading to the royal Palace, in fact a building above whose impressive gateway there runs a long covered balcony from which the Shah and his friends once watched the polo played in the Maidan.

While the two mosques on the Maidan were the great sights of Isfahan, the city had numerous other mosques, bridges, minarets and other buildings ornamented with the coloured mosaics of the local craftsmen. Among the oldest was the Friday Mosque or Masjid-i-Jami, parts of it dating back to the eleventh century. It was remarkable for the fact that the architects who later rebuilt the mosque solved the problem of setting a circular dome on a square base.

On the far outskirts of the town there were the famous 'shaking minarets', rising above the entrance to a small Mongol mosque. By pushing against one of the walls, it was possible to make one of the minarets oscillate; then, for reasons that are even now not quite clear, the second minaret also starts to oscillate.

The centre of Isfahan has been greatly altered since Shah Abbas' day. But many of the most important mosques have been carefully restored; the bright colours remain after the centuries; and across the Maidan the great gateway to the Shah Abbas Mosque, with its minarets and dome, still shimmers in the sun.

The Friday mosque (above left); *the Shaikh Luftallah mosque* (above right); *the Shah mosque and ceiling* (below left and right).

The Alhambra

The Alhambra — a corruption of 'Kal'at al hambra', meaning the red castle — is the ancient fortress and palace of the monarchs of Granada in southern Spain, and the most superb example of Moorish architecture in Europe.

From the hills outside the city it can be seen that the complex of gardens, pools and buildings has been laid out across a flat plateau whose steep approaches make it almost impregnable. These natural defences are reinforced by the red walls, once studded with 13 fortified towers, which enclose the 14 hectares (35 acres). In their own way, the gardens with their myrtles and oranges are as remarkable as the palace itself, containing waterfalls, fountains, and a small forest of elms planted there by the Duke of Wellington in 1812.

The Alhambra has had a turbulent history since the first defences were erected and the palace was begun by Ibn-l-ahmar in 1248 on what is a natural acropolis. It was not until 1314 that the elaborate work was completed by his grandson Mohammed III. Less than 200 years later the Moors were expelled, and with their expulsion there began a long reign of vandalism. Charles v rebuilt

St Basil's Cathedral

Opinions have always differed about the Cathedral of St Basil the Beatified, the extraordinary building in Moscow's Red Square. Theodore Gautier compared it to a giant piece of coral; others have called it a nightmare in stone, and the dream of a diseased imagination. At the other extreme it has been praised as an ultimate expression of true Russian architecture. But few who have gazed at its multicoloured domes and spires have been unmoved by the sight.

Originally known as the Cathedral of the Intercession of the Virgin, the building was commissioned by the young Tsar Ivan IV (Ivan the Terrible) following his victories over the Tartars of Kazan and Astrakhan. At the centre there was to be the main church while around it were to be grouped eight subsidiary churches, each with its own altar and ikons, and each dedicated to a saint whose feast day coincided with one of the Tsar's main victories over the enemy.

Two Russian architects were given the task in 1554. Six years later the building was finished, a construction of stucco-covered stone and brick which was originally painted white. Over the central church

there rose a steep tent-shaped roof, surmounted by a bulbous cupola. Surrounding it were four octagonal churches and four subsidiary churches of different shape. Above them rose cupolas finished into different forms; some resembled pineapples, some turbans, while others were finished with fanciful spiral ribbing designs.

If the shape of the building, with its separate parts rising sturdily from the Red Square, was enough to give the impression of 'a colossal plant', the painting of the stucco in the seventeenth century transformed it into a vividly coloured spectacle. One of the spires is decorated with spiralling bands of yellow and green, another with a green network upon red. Red, orange, violet, gold and silver enhance the walls and decorations and by contrast the interior is dark.

Today the cathedral, once famous for its colourful Palm Sunday processions, has been turned into a museum.

Above: *St Basil's, a 'giant piece of coral' or a 'nightmare in stone'?*

portions of the ornate buildings and destroyed the winter palace. Philip v italianized many of the rooms in the eighteenth century, covered up much of the wonderful Moorish inlaid work and transformed many of the interiors. After Philip, the Alhambra was commanded by a military Governor, but slowly began to fall into decay. It was saved partly by the French who during the Napoleonic Wars garrisoned the fortress. 'The roofs were repaired', said Washington Irving, the famous American writer who stayed in the fortress in the 1820s; 'the saloons and galleries [were] protected from the weather, the gardens cultivated, the watercourses restored, the fountains once more made to throw up their sparkling showers; and Spain may thank her invaders for having preserved to her the most beautiful and interesting of her historical monuments.'

On their departure, the French destroyed eight of the 13 defensive towers, but it was left to an earthquake in 1821 to do more serious damage. There followed some years of neglect but in 1862 Queen Isabella began a long-term plan of restoration work, the results of which can still be seen today.

Only the outer walls of the great citadel, or Alcazaba, still remain, but many of the superb courts and rooms have been brought back to something like their original magnificence. These include the

Court of the Lions paved with coloured tiles and, in its centre, the magnificent Lion fountain, with its alabaster basin supported by twelve marble lions; and the Court of the Myrtles with its long translucent pool. The most beautiful room in the palace is sometimes claimed to be the Hall of the Abencerrages whose colour and ornamentation is emphasized by an arcade of marble arches. The hall is named after the famous Abencerrages family who are claimed to have been wiped out by one of the last rulers of the Alhambra. According to legend the family was invited to a formal banquet in the Court of the Lions then called, one by one, into the hall now bearing their name. There, each was beheaded.

In addition to the larger rooms and courts, the palace contains a multiplicity of small courts, small gardens and mosaic pavements, all elaborately ornamented.

Below left: *The Mirador of Lindaraja, the Alhambra.*
Below right: *The Court of the Lions.*

Venice

Venice, an extraordinary city built on a few score mud-flats and islands, was once one of the most important trading centres in the world. Its wealth attracted the greatest painters, craftsmen and architects of Europe and today their work attracts pilgrims from all over the world. It does so, moreover, while a constant battle is being fought to keep Venice from the waters that were long ago its protection against invaders.

The first inhabitants of Venice, driven from the nearby mainland, settled on more

than 70 islets which cluster in a lagoon at the northern end of the Adriatic. Two miles to the west lies the Italian mainland, today joined to Venice by a narrow road and rail causeway; to the east the lagoon is partially closed by a narrow island strip in which there are three gaps through which the tides pour in and out every day. The archipelago of islets and islands is intersected by a maze of nearly 150 canals, the largest being the S-shaped Grand Canal which splits the archipelago into two. A network of narrow lanes runs along the canals, which are crossed by some 400 bridges so that all Venetian houses, palaces and churches can be reached on foot.

The earlier inhabitants laid stone and plank foundations for their buildings on the clay which was only a few feet below sea-level. Later builders used piling, but despite this the whole of Venice is now in danger from the waters.

The sub-stratum on which there have been built the great Basilica of St Mark, the Palace of the Doges, and the other magnificent buildings that have made Venice one of the artistic meccas of the world, is sinking at the rate of nine inches a century. This peril was dramatically underlined in November 1966 when the tide, rising 1·8 metres (6 ft) instead of its normal 0·5–1 metre (2–3 ft), inundated Venice and caused almost irreparable damage to many of its treasures.

The danger has been steadily increased since the end of the Second World War, partly by the use of power-boats whose wash tends to erode foundations, partly by the digging of artesian wells. But well-digging has now been outlawed and water is brought to the city by an aqueduct. Meanwhile, plans are going ahead for the construction of three water-gates which can be closed to seal off the lagoon from the waters of the Adriatic in time of danger.

Far left: The Piazza San Marco, seen from the terrace of the Basilica.

Below: Evening strollers enjoy the Venetian twilight. The spires of San Giorgio Maggiore dominate the view across the Grand Canal.

Neuschwanstein Castle

A mock-Gothic extravagance, built little more than a century ago by a king who was taken from its rooms after being declared insane by government doctors, Neuschwanstein Castle is one of the most extraordinary sights of southern Germany.

King Ludwig II came to the throne of Bavaria in 1864 at the age of 19. As a child his favourite games were with building bricks, and once he was granted sufficient money from the government he embarked on an orgy of castle-building. The most famous of these fairy-tale constructions was Neuschwanstein, standing on a precipitous crag above a deep ravine in the Algau Alps some 60 miles south-west of Munich and 20 from the modern ski resort of Garmisch-Partenkirschen.

Ludwig told his friend Wagner, the composer whose patron he was, that his plan was to rebuild the ruins of the ancient castle that still rested on the chosen spot. In fact, six metres (20 ft) was blasted off the top of the crag to provide a level place for a completely new castle to include a minstrels' hall inspired by the thirteenth-century minstrel Tannhäuser and a huge sitting room whose walls are covered with illustrations from the Lohengrin legend.

A plan was prepared by a court architect, Eduard Riedel, and by the scenic designer of a Munich theatre, and the foundation stone was laid in the late summer of 1869. The following year the outbreak of the Franco-Prussian war, in which Bavaria joined, failed to stop work and throughout the next decade the enormous building continued to take shape. The third floor, where the royal apartments start – the lower ones being occupied with offices and staff quarters – is reached by a huge staircase of 96 steps in the massive, 60-metre (195-ft) high, north tower. Beyond the Adjutant's room is the King's study, ornamented with scenes from Wagner's opera *Tannhäuser*. Beyond the study lies what was once called the Stalactite Grotto; a Winter Garden with a balcony commanding an extensive view of the surrounding country; and the Lohengrin sitting room.

The most remarkable room in the building is the arcaded Throne Room, modelled on a Byzantine basilica, extending through two floors, and with an ornate mosaic floor and walls covered with paintings showing the relationship between monarchy and religion. Next only to the Throne Room in magnificence is the 27-metre (90-ft) long Minstrels' Gallery.

The interior of Neuschwanstein Castle presents, in room after room, one of the most colourful sights of art and decoration anywhere in the world; its exterior, seen against the backdrop of forest, lake and mountain, has a fairy-tale quality of unreality. On 8 June 1886, its originator was declared insane by an official Medical Report – a verdict that today might be no more than a verdict of extreme eccentricity. Four days later he was forcibly removed from Neuschwanstein to Schloss Berg, 20 miles from Munich. The following day he was found drowned, probably the result of suicide, but in circumstances that have never been completely explained.

Below: *The mock-gothic extravaganza of Neuschwanstein Castle.*

Mont St Michel

Victor Hugo once said that Mont St Michel was to France what the pyramids were to Egypt, a bold claim that was in fact no exaggeration. Rising from the waters of the Baie de Mont St Michel, where Normandy meets Brittany, the Mount is an extraordinary rocky islet, a solitary cone of granite about 915 metres (3,000 ft) in circumference and 74 metres (242 ft) high, surrounded at high tide by calm waters and at low tide by a huge area of shimmering sand and quicksands that have claimed many lives. Only for the last 100 years has it been joined to the mainland by a mile-long causeway. Even more remarkable than the granite cone is the massive complex of buildings which today crowns the slopes, fortress as well as abbey and illustrating almost the entire course of Gothic architecture, military, domestic and ecclesiastical.

In Roman times, Mont St Michel was surrounded by dry land, much of it covered by the forest of Scissey which stretched as far as the Channel Islands. It had been crowned by a temple to Belen, the Celtic god of light, later turned into a shrine to the Roman god Mercury. In the third century, a general subsidence of the area brought the sea to the slopes of the cone. By the following century the Mount was isolated at high tide and could be reached from the mainland only by a dangerous passage marked out by tall stakes.

This isolation attracted the first permanent inhabitants: hermits who built on the summit two small oratories. They and their successors remained the only inhabitants of the island until early in the eighth century when St Aubert, Bishop of Avranches, the town 18 miles away down the coast, had a vision of St Michael the Archangel who ordered him to build a sanctuary on the mount. Numerous miracles are said to have helped on the work; thus a stolen cow showed where the first building was to be started; a babe in arms, held by the Bishop, removed a giant impeding boulder with a touch of his foot; and a second appearance of St Michael showed where fresh water could be found.

Shortly after the chapel-sanctuary had been completed a major inundation of the sea permanently isolated the mount which now became known as Mont St Michel-au-Peril-de-la-Mer. In 966 a Benedictine abbey was added and in the twelfth century this became a famous place of learning, giving the name 'City of Books' to the mass of buildings which now covered the island.

From the beginning of the thirteenth century additions were constantly made to the buildings on the Mount, notably the group still known as the 'Marvel of the

Western World', the monastery proper whose halls and chapels rise in perpendicular granite splendour from the natural rock. Throughout the Middle Ages Mont St Michel was not only a monastery to which pilgrims came from all over Europe but a fortress whose occupation was strongly and bloodily contested. During the latter part of the Hundred Years War its occupants, led by a secular Governor, beat off all attacks by the English. Between 1440 and 1450 it resisted a ten-year siege and during the Wars of Religion it held out against all the attacks of the Huguenots. Only in 1595, after Henry IV had been converted to Catholicism, did the monks surrender.

After the French Revolution the island – renamed Mount of Liberty – was turned into a prison, the first occupants of the cells being priests who had criticized the new regime. The great abbey halls were partitioned and the nave of the church was turned into a canteen and a workshop for

Above: The quiet beauty of Mont St Michel.

making hats. Only in the middle of the last century were serious efforts made to restore the buildings to their former glory. This task has long been completed and today the visitor can see the Norman nave and the Flamboyant choir; the unequalled Gothic cloisters; the Halle des Chevaliers where Louis XI founded the Order of St Michael in 1469; and 'La Merveille' with its huge supporting north wall.

On the lower slopes of the island there is today the tightly-packed knot of houses, facing each other across steeply-stepped narrow streets and lanes, many of them catering for the tourists who have replaced the pilgrims of earlier days. What draws them is not only the wonder of the extraordinary collection of Gothic architecture but the tide surging in across the sands of the bay – one of the most dramatic sights in all France.

The Stained Glass of Chartres Cathedral

Seen from the distance across flat fields, the twin spires and green roof of Chartres Cathedral dominate both the landscape and the city that surrounds it. Yet most visitors, prepared for something exceptional, are still astounded when they enter and accustom themselves to the extraordinary scene. Except on the most sunlit of days the interior is first dark if not gloomy. But as eyes become accustomed to the semi-darkness and as the patterns of light coming through the multi-coloured windows are changed by the passing clouds, the scene is illuminated by patches of green, red, orange and the richest purple.

The people of Chartres used to call the interior of their Cathedral 'La Forêt', and the writer Huysmans has described it as 'a forest blooming with roses of fire'. The significance of the words is seen to be true as the individual stained-glass windows are studied one by one. There are nearly 160 of them, including the two huge rose-windows, 9 and 12 metres (30 and 40 ft) across, at the ends of the nave and the transept. The present cathedral was built in 1194 to replace an earlier building destroyed by fire, and most of the windows were made in the city by teams of craftsmen during the thirteenth century.

Almost until the end of the twelfth century stained glass was mostly of a subtly different character. But about the turn of the century, craftsmen began to produce windows which under ideal conditions let in light which appeared more intense than that let in by earlier windows. The greens, reds and purples glowed and did, indeed, give the impression of light filtering down through the trees into the depths of a great forest. The new techniques continued for roughly 50 years, as the great walls and pillars of Chartres were being raised, and today its windows provide a unique example of medieval craftsmanship.

Most of the windows illustrate biblical subjects or legends of the saints. Some were paid for by trade guilds or corporations, the basket-makers or the shoemakers, as is shown by small details at the foot of some of the windows. Others were paid for by nobles such as the Count of Chartres, or by King Louis the Holy, who like the guilds, had their contributions acknowledged by their coats-of-arms or other identifying symbols.

Far right: *The rose and lancet windows of the north transept and two details (*King Saul, *above;* a pharaoh, *below) from the base of the lancet window.*

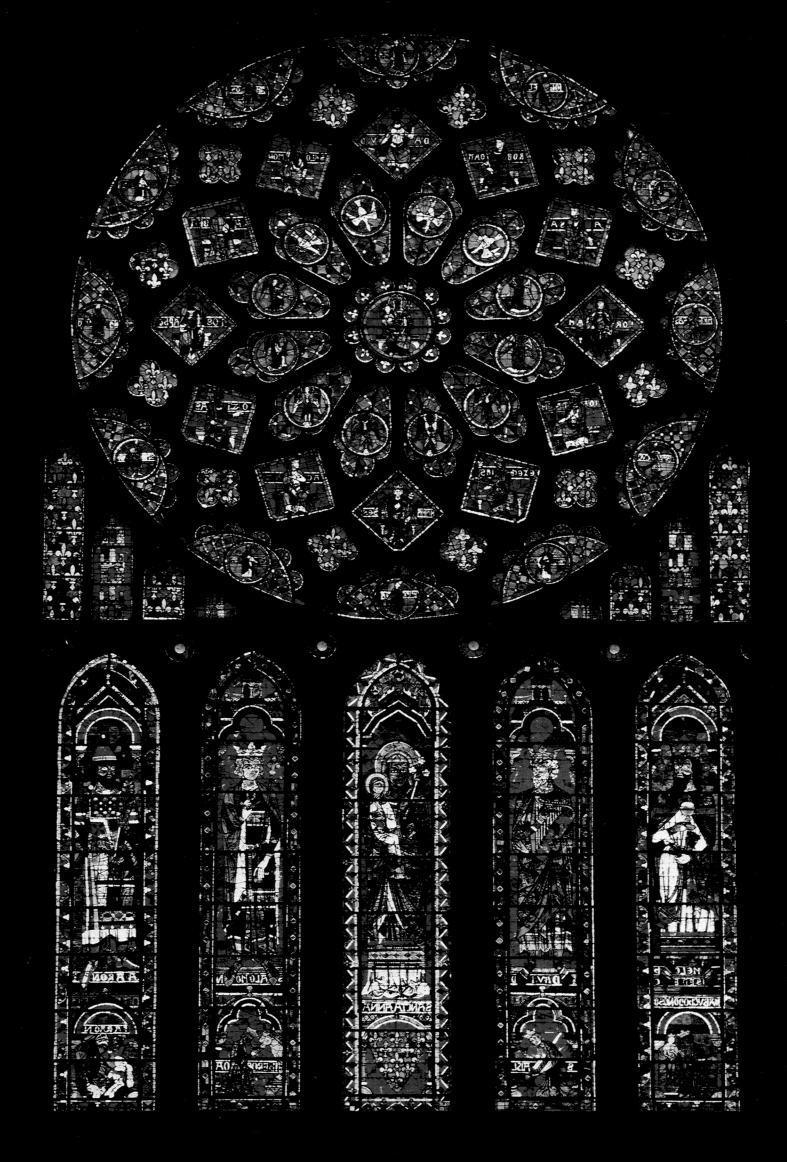

Radiotelescopes

Radio waves which came into existence many millions of years before the earth began are today being picked up by radiotelescopes and providing fresh clues to the age and nature of the universe. Although there are many kinds of radiotelescopes operating in Britain, the United States, Russia and Australia, the 2,500-ton fully-steerable giant at Jodrell Bank, outside Manchester, the creation of Sir Bernard Lovell, is the most famous of all.

Until the 1930s the light emitted by other bodies in the universe, and collected in optical telescopes, was man's only source of information about other bodies in our own solar system, in the galaxy (or collection of stars) of which the solar system forms part, and in the immense number of other galaxies which make up the universe. However, in 1931 and 1932 Karl Janský, working in the United States for the Bell Telephone Company, picked up on his radio equipment bursts of waves coming from sources beyond the solar system.

Little notice was taken of Jansky's observations, although one American, Grote Weber, built a small nine-metre (30-ft) receiver, confirmed Jansky's work and began to make a 'radio map' of the sky showing the directions from which various emissions appeared to be coming. By 1945, the development of radar had vastly increased the effectiveness of equipment for receiving radio waves and scientists began to discover how much the waves from distant space could tell them about the universe.

It quickly became clear that while the atmosphere and the ionosphere – the charged layer of the atmosphere from 50 to 150 miles above the earth – blocked the reception of some radio waves from outer space, those in the waveband from one centimetre to 10 metres (0·4 in–33 ft) passed through what has been described as a 'radio window'. One result was that scientists could probe out and 'see' bodies so distant that their light could not be registered on optical telescopes. Radio waves from more distant emitters have now been used by radio astronomers to estimate the density of matter in distant space, and, in 1957, to record the passage

of the first Russian sputnik with an accuracy which would have been impossible a few years earlier. Since then satellites from many countries have been regularly tracked by the laboratory. To measure the distance of the moon more accurately than ever before, a transmitter sent out radio waves which were bounced back to Jodrell Bank, the time for the double journey giving the distance travelled.

Among the more exciting discoveries of radio-astronomy are those of quasars and pulsars. The first of these – quasi-stellar radio sources – are extra-galactic sources of high energy, apparently receding from our own galaxy at immense speeds and thus supporting the theory of a constantly expanding universe. Pulsars are pulsating stars which emit radio waves in very brief pulses at extremely regular intervals.

Below: *The radiotelescope at Jodrell Bank, Cheshire, used to record the passage around the earth of the first Russian sputnik.*

Odeillo Solar Oven

High up in the French Pyrenees, a battery of mirrors is simulating the schoolboy trick of setting leaves alight by focusing sunlight on them with a magnifying glass – and is giving France the prospect of power from the sun within the next few years.

France has a long tradition of research into solar energy, starting with the naturalist Georges Louis Buffon who in 1747 used 140 mirrors in his Paris home to set alight a pile of wood 60 metres (200 ft) away. Antoine Lavoisier did much the same nearly 30 years later and devised a method of turning his mirrors by hand so that they could constantly remain pointing towards the sun. Today France has two organizations – the Solar Energy Committee and the Solar Energy Commission – co-

ordinating the research that the CNRS [Centre National de Recherche Scientifique] began soon after the end of the Second World War.

The first work was carried out at Mont-Louis, a small resort in the eastern Pyrenees and only a few miles from the frontier with Spain. Here, nearly 1,830 metres (6,000 ft) up, the sun shines about 180 days a year, and operations were so encouraging that it was planned to erect a larger device at nearby Odeillo.

On the fields outside what is in winter a popular ski-resort there was built in 1970 the curious erection that has brought results good enough for the French to plan a full-scale solar power station at Ajaccio on the island of Corsica. The most prominent feature of the solar oven is a huge parabolic reflector standing 40 metres (130 ft) high and consisting of 9,500 mirrors. Sunlight is reflected on to this array by a group of 63 flat mirrors and is then, in turn,

Above: *Part of the huge mirror-system at Odeillo.*

concentrated on to a 'target' nearly 18 metres (60 ft) away. But while the parabolic mirror is stationary, the other 63 mirrors can be automatically steered for up to eight hours a day so that they constantly give maximum efficiency. Temperatures of up to 3,800°C (6,872°F) can be obtained in the 'target' area and during the last 10 years the Odeillo furnace has been used for a great deal of thermal research.

The French have an ambitious national plan for exploiting solar energy in various different ways; are encouraging its use in agriculture and industry, as well as in houses; and hope that by the end of the century it will be providing five per cent of the country's energy requirements, thus saving the equivalent of 17 million tons of oil.

Nuclear Energy

Nuclear energy is released when the nuclei of certain heavy atoms, notably those of the rarest kind of uranium, are split into two parts; or when the nuclei of certain kinds of hydrogen are made to join. The first, the fission process, can be uncontrolled as in the atomic bomb or controlled as in nuclear power stations; the second has, as yet, only been demonstrated in the un-controlled process used in the hydrogen bomb.

During the nineteenth century it was believed that atoms were solid, hard and indivisible, rather like extremely small billiard balls. During the last 70 and more years, however, it has been found that atoms have a nucleus consisting of positively-charged particles called protons and non-charged particles called neutrons, while surrounding the nucleus there are circling negatively-charged particles called electrons. Atoms of different materials – or elements as they are called – differ in size and in number of particles but are all something like a hundred-millionth of an inch across. This means that 100,000 atoms placed on top of each other would make up the thickness of a cigarette paper.

Splitting, or nuclear fission, takes place when a metal such as uranium 235 – which has a total of 235 protons and neutrons in its nucleus – is bombarded with neutrons. If a nucleus absorbs a neutron it becomes unstable, and then splits into two parts. The masses of these two parts add up to less than the mass of the original nucleus and fly apart with the release of an enormous amount of energy. This energy is, weight for weight, roughly a million times greater than the energy released by such chemical transformations as the burning of wood or coal.

Even more important is the fact that when the uranium nucleus splits into two it releases a small number of 'free' neutrons. These in turn can cause further fissioning in a block of uranium, thus starting a chain-reaction or nuclear fire.

In the release of nuclear energy for peaceful purposes such as power-production in a nuclear reactor, the chain-reaction can be controlled in two ways. One is by the use of a moderator, which may be graphite, heavy water (water whose composition is different from that of ordinary water), or a number of other substances. Secondly, a nuclear reactor uses a number of control rods which contain boron, cadmium or some other strong absorber of neutrons. These rods can be pushed deeper into the reactor if too much energy is being created, or pulled out if the amount is too little.

The heat produced in the reactor by fission is transferred to a gas, to water, or to liquid metal, which is continuously cir-culated around it; this operates a steam

generator, which in turn drives a turbine which produces electricity.

The utilization of nuclear energy in the 1950s presented immense engineering and chemical difficulties. These have now been largely overcome, although the safe disposal of the radioactive wastes produced by fission is still a problem that has not been satisfactorily solved.

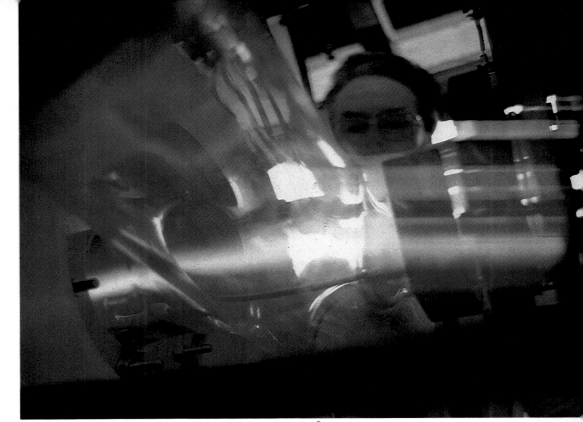

Above right: *Plasma containment research into nuclear fusion.*

Below left: *The fuel assembly for a gas-cooled nuclear reactor.*

Below right: *Equipment used to inspect the fuel rods in a nuclear power station.*

Accelerator Rings

Among all the wonders of modern science, few are more extraordinary than the latest accelerator rings, huge contrivances which increase the speed of nuclear particles until they are travelling at more than 200,000 miles per second. The rings, metal tubes in which almost unimaginably small particles can be subjected to measurable forces, cost many millions of pounds to build and are the descendants of the 'atom-smashers' used before the Second World War to investigate the way in which atomic nuclei are built.

The aim of the accelerators is to 'shoot' particles towards a target at as high a velocity as possible. If the speed is great enough the particles which hit the target shatter nuclei in the target material; and from the speed, trajectory and weight of the fragments into which these break – all automatically recorded – it is possible to learn more about their structure.

Until about 40 years ago it was believed that there were only three kinds of particle, the positively-charged proton, the non-charged neutron in the nucleus, and a third type, the negatively-charged electron, orbiting the nucleus in various numbers. Today, atomic structure is known to be much more complicated, and sub-atomic particles of more than 100 different kinds have been discovered, some of them existing for only a fraction of a second.

In the first accelerators, a high voltage was applied directly to the particles which were to be speeded up. This was true of the original Van de Graaf accelerator, made in Princeton, New Jersey in 1929, and of the apparatus with which John Cockcroft and E.T.S. Walton split the atomic nucleus with speeded-up particles in Cambridge in 1932.

In the same year E.O. Lawrence of Berkeley, California, built the world's first cyclotron, an apparatus in which the particles to be speeded up were 'pushed on' by successive additions of energy. This was done by using a magnetic field to make the particles traverse a spiral path between two semi-circular electrodes called 'dees'. At each half-revolution between the dees the particles received an additional charge, the last addition being made just before the spiral route ended at the target.

Contemporary accelerator rings such as those at the CERN [Conseil Européen pour la Recherche Nucléaire] Laboratory in Geneva, at the Brookhaven National Laboratory on Long Island and at Stanford University in California, use circular underground tunnels, a mile or more in circumference, in which particles are accelerated by a variety of methods. At the Fermilab accelerator in Batavia, Illinois, particles are already being accelerated to enormous velocities in a tunnel some four miles in length. After travelling round the tunnel at a rate of about 50,000 times per second, the particles hit their target with an energy of some 500 billion electron-volts – enough, that is, to melt a hole in a steel beam.

Below: *The spiral of the Cockcroft-Walton ion accelerator, one of the early pieces of equipment used to speed up nuclear particles. A later model based on the original.*

The Alaskan Pipeline

In 1968 American engineers struck oil on the bleak North Slope of Alaska, the barren country deep within the Arctic Circle stretching from the Brook Mountain Range to the shores of the Arctic Ocean itself. Beneath the frozen landscape, it was estimated, there lay no less than 10,000,000,000,000 barrels of oil – as much as the combined reserves of Louisiana, Oklahoma, Kansas and half of Texas. The problem lay not so much in drilling for it as in getting it to the bustling industrial centres of North America many thousands of miles away.

Transport by road, it was worked out, would require a fleet of 60,000 tanker vehicles operating round the clock, seven days a week, 365 days a year. Moving the oil out by rail would demand the building of two sets of tracks, one for the loaded waggons going out and the other for their return, empty. Even then, it was estimated,

Above: *The Alaskan pipeline crossing the Tanana River, south-east of Fairbanks, Alaska.*

one 100-waggon train would have to leave the oilfields every 23 minutes of the day and night.

The companies involved then investigated an audacious idea: that of building an 800-mile pipeline from Prudhoe Bay on the shores of the Arctic Ocean, through some of the most desolate country in the world, much of it perpetually frozen hard, to the ice-free port of Valdez on the southern coast of Alaska. The pipeline would have to traverse the 1,463-metre (4,800-ft) Dietrich Pass of the Brooks Range, cross the 708 metre (2,300 ft) wide Yukon River, climb to the 1,067-metre (3,500-ft) Isabel Pass of the Alaska Mountain Range, cross the Copper River, and rise another 762 metres (2,500 ft). Only then would it descend through the Keystone Canyon to the port of Valdez. Much of the route would be over territory where permafrost held the ground in its grip throughout the year and the temperature could fall to −62°C (−80°F); yet on the southern sections of the route the summer temperature might rise to 32°C (90°F). If all this did not produce difficult enough conditions,

parts of the route were known to be subject to earthquakes. And with up to two million barrels of oil moving daily it was obvious that a single fracture could produce an ecological disaster.

Despite the problems, oil began to flow through the pipe from Prudhoe Bay to Valdez in the summer of 1977, a signal that one of the New World's great engineering ventures was a success. 1·2 metres (4 ft) in diameter and roughly 13 mm ($\frac{1}{2}$ in) in thickness, the pipe had been made in three different minimum yield strengths and tested to ensure its safety in the worst conceivable conditions. A computer at Valdez receives a continuous flow of information from points along the line, the entire line can be shut down in six minutes if necessary, and emergency crews are on a permanent standby basis. These are among the special precautions taken to ensure that if there is an unexpected emergency any damage will be strictly limited.

There have been fears that the pipeline, and the impact of the construction crews, might seriously affect the environment. However, although up to 10,000 men were

employed to build the pipeline only about 300 are now needed to operate, monitor and maintain it. Moreover no one connected with the oil industry or the pipeline is allowed to hunt the wildlife while working on the project. Huge quantities of gravel had to be taken from the rivers which the pipeline crosses, both for foundation material and for the highway. If this had been extracted while fish were migrating or were in or upstream of the spawning areas, there could have been great damage to the valuable salmon stocks. Extraction was therefore limited to a few weeks, and during these the workers had to remove a whole year's requirements.

So far, it appears that only minimum impact has been made on the great Alaskan wilderness, today one of America's great assets. Only the future will show whether this continues to be true.

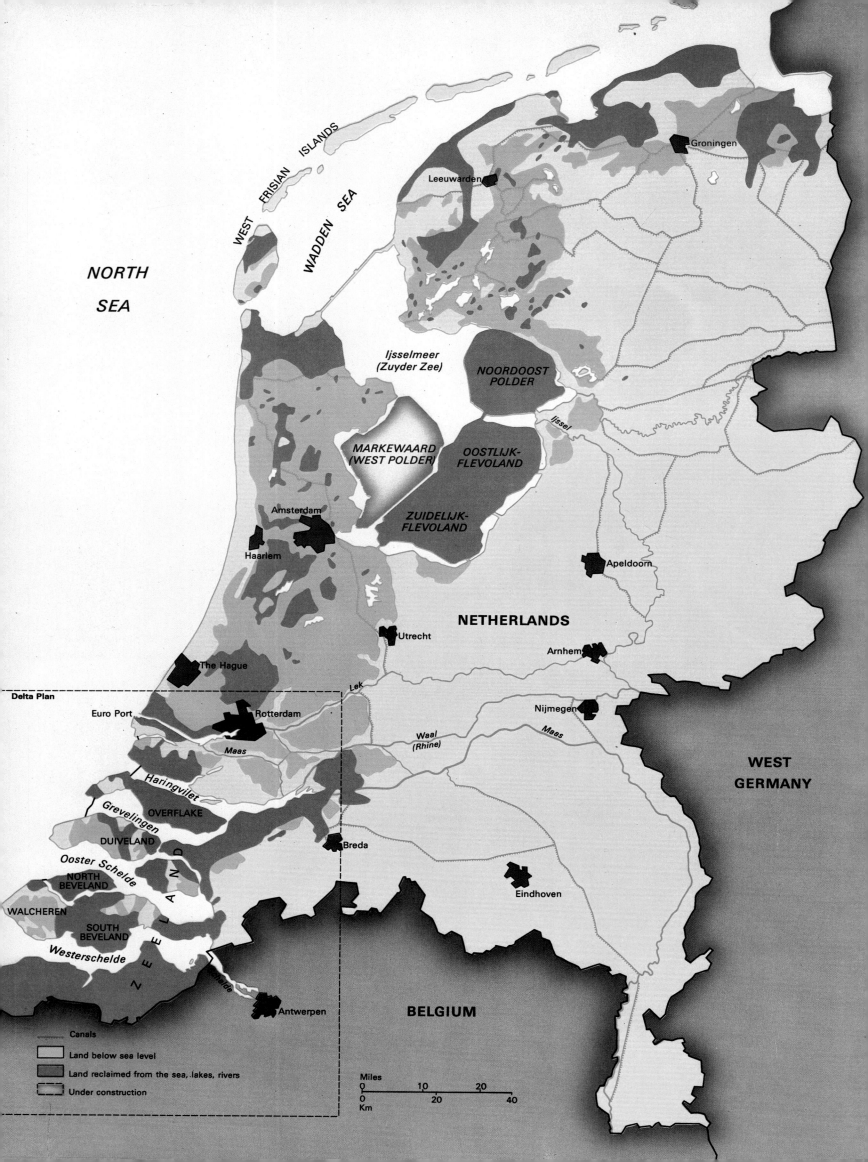

NORTH
SEA

WADDEN SEA

WEST FRISIAN ISLANDS

Groningen

Leeuwarden

Ijsselmeer
(Zuyder Zee)

NOORDOOST
POLDER

Ijssel

MARKEWAARD
(WEST POLDER)

OOSTLIJK-
FLEVOLAND

ZUIDELIJK-
FLEVOLAND

Amsterdam

Haarlem

Apeldoorn

NETHERLANDS

Utrecht

Arnhem

The Hague

Delta Plan

Euro Port

Rotterdam

Lek

Maas

Nijmegen

Waal
(Rhine)

Maas

WEST
GERMANY

Haringvliet

Grevelingen

OVERFLAKE

Breda

DUIVELAND

Ooster Schelde

NORTH
BEVELAND

Eindhoven

WALCHEREN

SOUTH
BEVELAND

Westerschelde

Z E E L A N D

Schelde

Antwerpen

BELGIUM

Canals

Land below sea level

Land reclaimed from the sea, lakes, rivers

Under construction

Miles
0   10   20

0   20   40
Km

Holland's Delta Plan

On 27 April 1961, the fishermen of the Dutch town of Veere, lying on the northern side of Walcheren Island, watched an amazing sight. For generations they and their ancestors had used the incoming tides as an unfailing daily clock. But on that April day the unbelievable happened: the waters failed to reach high-tide mark. The reason was that the first stage in an engineering wonder of the western world had been completed. A few miles to seaward the last of seven giant concrete caissons had been towed into place and then sunk in the Veerschegat, one of the waterways through which the River Scheldt pours into the North Sea and up which the tides had flowed since before man first came to the Netherlands. The Dutch had taken one more step in transforming their country.

The historic event was part of the Delta Plan, a massive and successful engineering project aimed at altering the face of nature,

inaugurated a few weeks after the great sea disaster of 1953. In that year, on the night of 31 January, the North Sea had inundated the Dutch province of Zeeland, smashing through the dams and dykes, drowning nearly 2,000 inhabitants and making many more thousands homeless. The Dutch, determined that the tragedy should not be repeated, had within a year started work on a project that was to change the landscape of the south-west Netherlands.

From the dawn of history the Dutch had been fighting the sea. Almost from pre-historic times they had built numbers of raised artificial mounds or islands – known as 'terps' – higher than the general land level and covering many acres. The next step was to join these mounds by dykes, on the inland side of which there lay the low-lying polders (pieces of land reclaimed from seas or rivers). These were drained of the flood-waters that sometimes breached the dykes in bad weather, first by windmills which were used to move the water back to the sea, later by steam pumps. During the first half of the present century the Dutch built a dam across the entrance of

the Zuyder Zee, the great gulf that stretches 60 miles into the country, and began the draining of the polders inside.

Impressive as this land reclamation was, it paled beside the Delta Plan on which thousands of workers were employed during the 1960s and '70s. The scheme first involved building storm barrages in the lower reaches of the rivers Rhine and Scheldt. Below these reaches the rivers spread out into the delta in which lie the islands of south and north Beveland, of Duiveland and of Overflakke; the key to success lay in joining up the seaward extremities of these islands with dams over which the seas could never break. Then the artificial polders behind them could be reclaimed.

The building of these dams, the most important being some eight miles long, presented immense engineering problems since they had to be built, in effect, in the open sea. The task would have been impossible but for various technical devices developed during the Second World War. The most important of these was the huge concrete caisson, numbers of which were used to build the artificial 'Mulberry' harbours off the coast of Normandy in the summer of 1944. Dozens of these concrete monsters were now re-designed and built, towed into position and then sunk as the foundation of the dams. Brushwood mattresses had previously been used to protect the sea-beds from the effect of new dams, but the enormous quantities required by the Delta Plan went far beyond Holland's resources, so mattresses of nylon were devised and laid where necessary with special machinery. New vessels were designed for underwater asphalting and for laying immense quantities of stone. And where sluices had to be opened a computer processed information on water levels, wind direction, and wave height and then automatically opened the sluices at the right moment.

Now, behind the dams, the face of southern Holland is changing. The fishing and shell-fish industries are giving way to new occupations and by the end of the century agriculture will have taken over in many places. And by that time the Dutch are expected to have started on their next great venture to protect their country from the North Sea – the Wadden Sea Project. This will link up the Frisian Islands, which curve round in an arc to the north of the Netherlands coastline, and turn them into a fresh barrier protecting the Dutch from the waves.

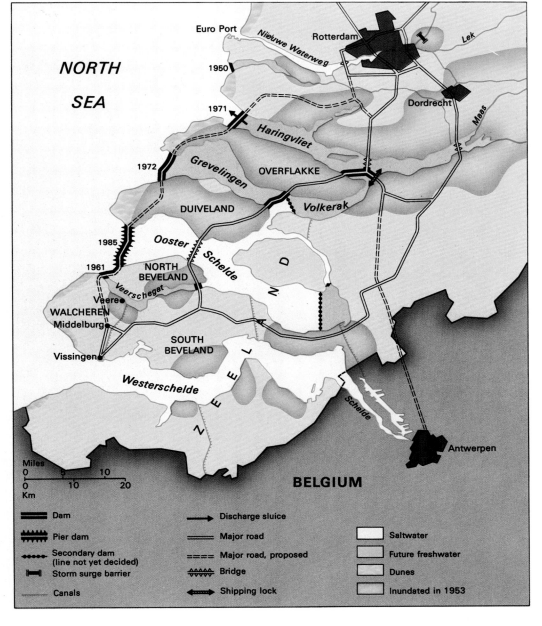

Legend	
Dam	Discharge sluice
Pier dam	Major road
Secondary dam (line not yet decided)	Major road, proposed
Storm surge barrier	Bridge
Canals	Shipping lock
	Saltwater
	Future freshwater
	Dunes
	Inundated in 1953

Far left: *Extensive areas of Holland have been reclaimed, particularly around the Zuyder Zee.*

Left: *The Delta Plan in the southwest, with its complex of dams, bridges and canals.*

Voyager Probes

Man's most ambitious attempt to explore the solar system began on 20 August 1977 when Voyager I, a three-quarter-ton spacecraft, was blasted off from Cape Canaveral on a journey that may last twelve years and take it to Neptune, the planet which is more than 2,000 million miles away. Sixteen days later Voyager II blasted off as the second half of the two-spaceship mission which represents a modern miracle of technology. When the rockets cut off to end powered flight each craft was travelling at nearly nine miles a second.

The Voyager mission's task is to investigate Jupiter, which the spacecraft passed in March and July, 1979, then Saturn in 1980 and 1981. After that they may be directed to the planet Uranus and its five moons, and then on to the huge planet Neptune. This will only be possible because the four planets Jupiter, Saturn, Uranus and Neptune will by that time be aligned with the earth, something that happens only once in 190 years.

Earlier space missions to Mars, Venus, Mercury and the Moon have already provided much information on the solar system. However, these are bodies consisting mainly of the heavier elements; the more distant planets are very different and are of low average density, being composed mainly of hydrogen and helium. They are big enough to suggest that they have retained almost all their original material since they began to evolve almost five billion years ago.

The spaceships, which carry cameras, infrared and ultraviolet spectrometers, and low-field magnetometers among a mass of other scientific instruments, are different from the earlier Mariner spaceships with which America's National Aeronautics and Space Administration began its exploration of the solar system.

Around Jupiter sunlight is only 1/25th as bright as around the earth, while around Uranus it is only 1/350th. So instead of the solar cells which in earlier spacecraft converted sunlight to electricity, the Voyagers rely on radioisotope thermogenerators which use the radioactive decay of uranium to produce heat and then electricity.

Unlike Mariners, the Voyagers do not use a single main rocket engine to correct their trajectory through space. Instead, they use hydrazine rocket propellant in 16 small thrusters. These enable the craft to be manoeuvred as required, and positioned by reference to the Sun and the star Canopus, or by the use of their own gyroscopes which provide an inertial reference system.

The Voyagers carry two sets of antennae for transmission of information to the earth. With the help of these it is possible for each of the spacecraft to send 115,000 'bits' of information per second from the area of Jupiter and 44,000 from the area of Saturn – a 'bit' being the unit of information needed to specify one of two alternatives, such as one and zero. By contrast the ordinary telephone can only carry 100 'bits' per second.

The information sent back by the Voyagers during the investigation of Jupiter

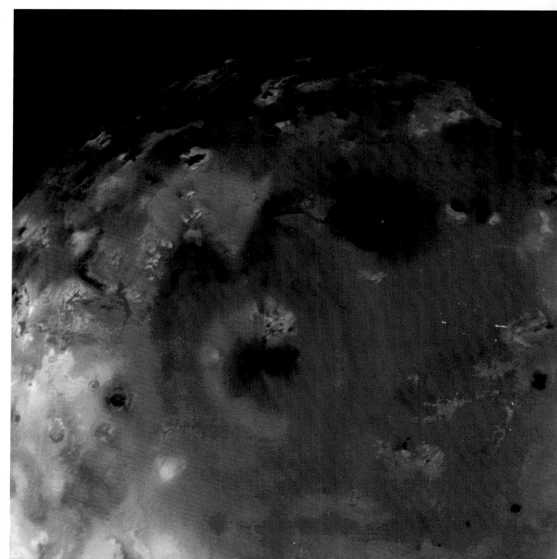

Jupiter and its satellites photographed early in 1979 by Voyager I.

Far right: *Jupiter with its Great Red Spot (bottom left) and its satellite Io (brown-yellow, towards right of planet) taken from 17·5 million miles.*

Above right: *A close-up of the planet's Great Red Spot and its surroundings, taken from 5·7 million miles away.*

Below right: *Io from 266,200 miles.*

in 1979 was much more than it had ever been possible to obtain from earth. Some of the most surprising data gave details of a giant ring of particles circling Jupiter about 33,000 miles above the planet's atmosphere; but although some 4,000 miles wide, the ring is only a mile thick. The spaceships also gave the first close photographs of Amalthea, the innermost of Jupiter's satellites, and examined four of the planet's big satellites, Io, Europa, Ganymede and Callisto.

A total of 11 different kinds of experiment are being carried out by the Voyagers. These can be divided into three different groups. The optical scanners collect information enabling scientists to understand the physical form or chemical composition of the planets and their satellites. A second group is designed to produce information on the planets' magnetic fields. A third set will monitor radio emissions from the planets and will investigate the characteristics of waves in the plasma surrounding them. The outcome of these experiments will, it is hoped, increase man's understanding of the solar system and its origin and evolution.

At the end of the mission the Voyagers will continue travelling until they leave the area of 43 planets and moons controlled by the sun which we know as the solar system. But, barring accidents, men on earth will be able to receive messages from the Voyagers for a total of 30 years, by which time they will be 9,300 million miles away.

The Space-Shuttle

A decisive step will be taken when the American space-shuttle starts its journey in the 1980s, thus making travel in space feasible not only for 'physically-perfect astronauts' but for what the US National Aeronautics and Space Administration calls reasonably healthy men and women.

The craft that makes this possible is shot from the Earth's orbit as a rocket, manoeuvres in orbit as a space-ship, and lands like an aircraft. Designed in the early 1970s when the Americans were investigating the idea of permanently-manned platforms in space, the vehicle consists of an Orbiter which in shape and size is not unlike a commercial air transport and can carry as many as seven crew; an external tank which at lift-off contains about one-and-a-half million gallons of liquid hydrogen and liquid oxygen as fuel for the Orbiter's three rocket-engines; and two solid-fuel booster rockets. With the exception of the external tank, all these components can be used again and again, and around 500 Shuttle missions are envisaged for the 1980s.

The varied tasks for which the space-shuttle can be used include work in weather forecasting, mapping, oceanography and navigation. It can be used to put into earth orbit such satellites as the Space Telescope now being completed. It can, at short notice, provide a vantage point in

space for observing transient astronomical events, or unexpected weather, agricultural or environmental crises. And it can carry into space the complete scientific laboratory developed by the European Space Agency and known as 'Spacelab'. Belgium, Denmark, France, Italy, the Netherlands, Spain, Switzerland, the United Kingdom and West Germany have all participated in Spacelab while Austria is an observer country.

Perhaps more spectacularly the Orbiter will be able to carry into orbit the components out of which will be made self-sustaining settlements. Their inhabitants will not only be able to build and maintain solar power stations but will use the unusual characteristics of weightlessness to create new alloys, produce unusually pure drugs and optical lenses, and grow crystals of giant size.

In a typical shuttle mission, which could last from a week to a month, the Shuttle will blast off either from the John F. Kennedy Space Center in Florida (for east-west orbits) or from the Vandenberg Air Force Base, California (for polar or north-south orbits). Those on board will experience a gravity load of only 3 G, which is roughly a third of that experienced on previous manned flights into space. At a height of about 42·5 km (140,000 ft) the two booster rockets will fall away. As they do so, parachutes will open and the empty boosters will fall into the ocean and float until collected for further use.

The Orbiter will continue its ascent until,

at between 60 and 70 miles up, it will go into preliminary orbit as the external tank is discarded. This will burn itself up on re-entry into the earth's atmosphere. Meanwhile, the Orbiter's manoeuvring engines will put it into circular orbit at anything from 110 to 700 miles above the earth.

When its mission is completed the craft's manoeuvring engines will be used to slow it down. As the speed falls the craft will drop lower and finally re-enter the earth's atmosphere. This will almost certainly be the most critical time for the whole operation since the craft, without its own power now, has but one chance of making a successful landing. To make things less difficult the crew will be able to manoeuvre the craft as much as 1,100 miles to left or right of its orbit, while the most sophisticated automatic landing system will be used to bring it on to the 4,572-metre (15,000-ft) runway at Cape Canaveral. Here, as on blast-off, the gravity load, at 1·5 G, will be only about a third of that experienced on previous manned space-flights.

The 'Shuttle Era' as it is already being called, offers opportunities for a vast extension of man's activities in 'inner space' – but it also offers them far more economically than was previously thought possible.

Opposite: *Preparations for a space-shuttle launch from the back of a 747 cargo plane at the Dryden Flight Research Center, California, and the mid-air take-off* (above).

Masers and Lasers

The extraordinary results which can be obtained from masers (Microwave Amplification by Stimulated Emission of Radiation) and lasers (Light Amplification by Stimulated Emission of Radiation) are the result of one thing: the way in which the devices convert the energy existing in all matter into electromagnetic waves by the stimulation of other electromagnetic waves which are fed into it. The difference between masers and lasers is that the first operates at microwave frequencies, the second at optical frequencies – those of light.

Two electromagnetic waves are directed on to the heart of the device, one being the wave to be amplified. The second, known as the 'pumping' wave, excites the atoms in the chosen source – in the case of the ruby laser the atoms of chromium which give the gem its red colour. However, these atoms are unable to absorb the energy of the pumping wave and this energy is transferred to the first wave which is then emitted in a vastly strengthened form.

The idea of stimulated emission was conceived by Albert Einstein during the First World War, but it was not until 1953 that the first maser was produced in America It was quickly followed by the laser, in this case a small cylinder of ruby whose internal energy was excited by an encircling flash-tube and from whose end there was produced a narrow but very pure and concentrated beam of infrared light. Most light-sources produce beams which diverge, and even a searchlight beam, concentrated as it is by a convex mirror, begins to spread out after a comparatively short distance. But a laser beam, directed at the moon a quarter of a million miles away, would be only two miles across when it reached the planet's surface.

This coherence, as it is called, combined with intensity and the fact that laser beams consist of light of only one wavelength – in other words, of only one colour – have enabled them to be used for a surprisingly large number of equally surprising jobs. Lasers have been used for painlessly erasing birthmarks and tattoo marks. They have been incorporated in devices for mapping the moon and for finger-print identification, while they have many applications in extremely accurate range-finding, including one in which a laser emitter in an aircraft measures the build-up in wave-height on the ocean below.

A laser cane has been developed for the blind with a 'rangefinder' which can be adjusted between 0·9 metres (3 ft) and 3·6 metres (12 ft), and which gives warning of any obstructions ahead, including steps.

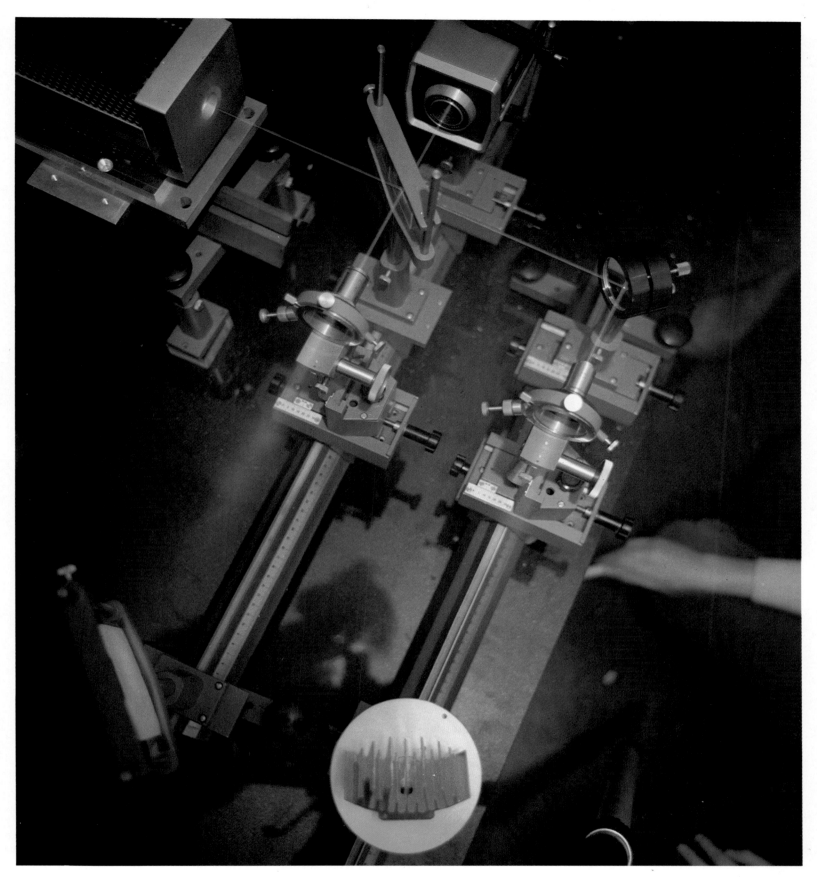

Many surgical uses have been developed, most of them based on the fact that a laser beam can burn out an extremely small area with only a minimum effect on surrounding parts of the body. Precision-cutting is one of the jobs which lasers can do; in the United States they have been applied to rock-tunnelling and aspects of coal-mining.

For technical reasons lasers can be used to carry far more messages, far more easily, than radio-waves and their use in communications systems is still being de-veloped. Perhaps the most fantastic potential for lasers is that of the system officially referred to by the US Senate Judiciary Subcommittee on Administration Practice and Procedure. This system could allegedly translate vibrations of a window into voice signals. Legal restraints on eavesdropping, it was noted, were based on the principles of trespass. But the laser beam in the system would bounce back off the window and reveal the conversation inside without trespassing into the room itself.

Opposite: *A laser beam at work, cutting through thick piles of cloth without distorting them.*

Above: *Equipment for using lasers to produce holographs, three-dimensional images obtained without the use of cameras or lenses.*

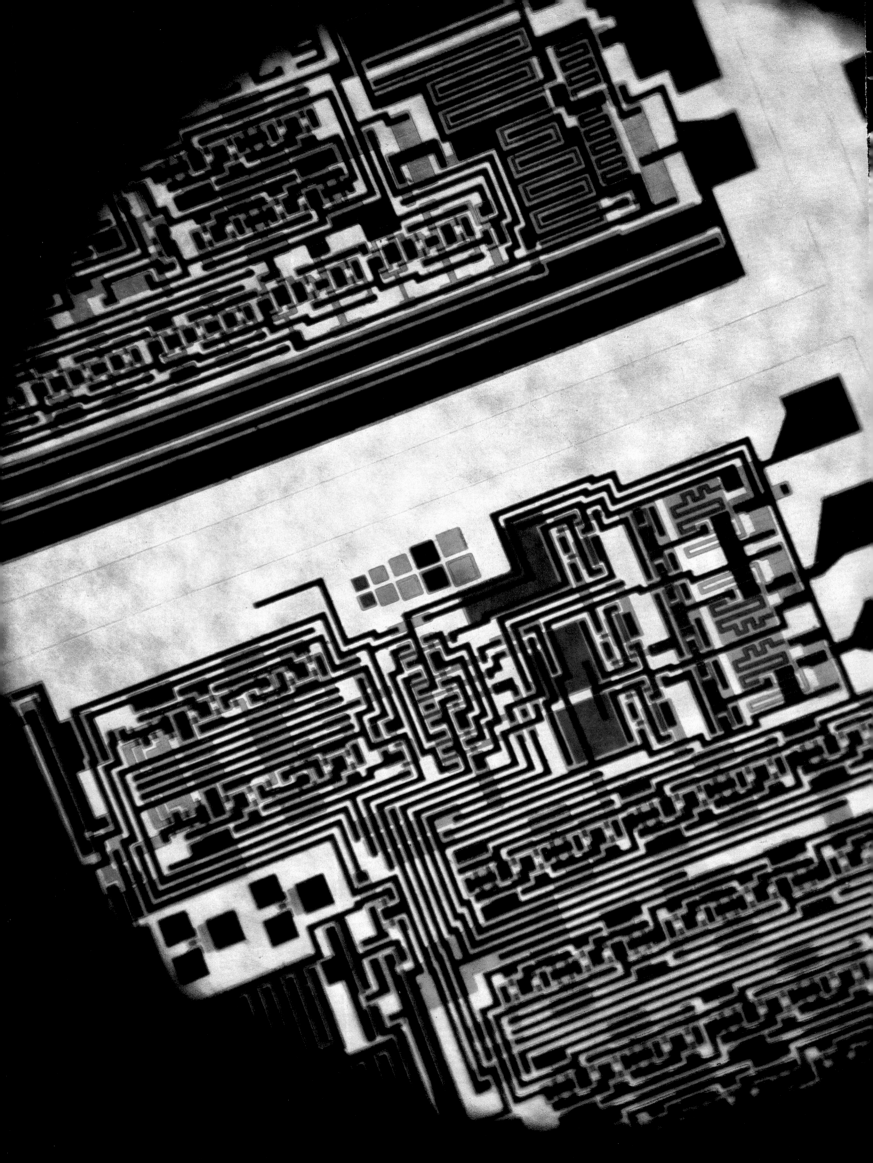

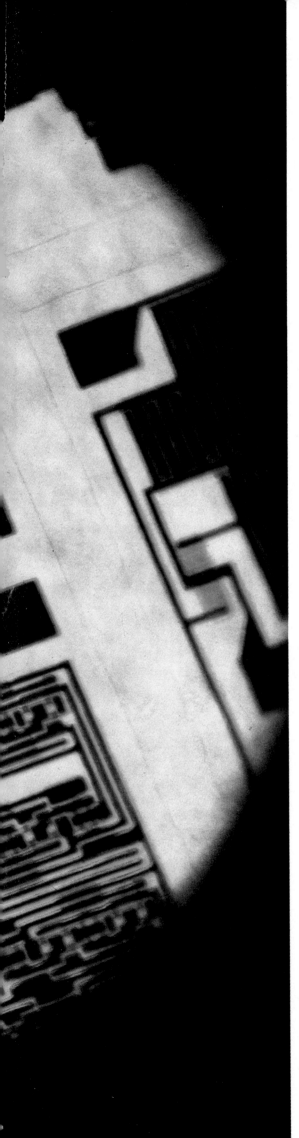

Silicon Chips

For many people, the silicon chip is the ultimate in twentieth-century technology – and with good reason, for the contemporary 'chip', only a few millimetres either way, can do the job of 16,000 transistors, the small solid-state devices that after the Second World War began to replace the thermionic valve of the early wireless days.

Transistors came into being from the development of certain materials known as semi-conductors, and including germanium, selenium and silicon, the last being the second most abundant element in the earth's crust. Semi-conductors, it was found, could be made to convert alternating current into direct current, and to amplify the current. This meant that they could do the job of the thermionic valve although they weighed less, were much smaller and consumed far less current. As electronic computers were developed, transistors quickly took over from the thousands of valves with the result that computers became less heavy, less bulky and less heat-producing.

Then, in the 1970s, new industrial techniques made it possible to form on a wafer-thin sliver of a semi-conductor such as silicon a pattern that interconnects such electronic devices as diodes, transistors, resistors and similar components. Electrical paths among these are either formed in the silicon or deposited on it in thin aluminium or gold layers. Manufacture involves the use of expensive precision machinery, fully controlled chemical processes and an extremely complex technology in which the chip area is exposed to different chemicals, to ultra-violet light, to ion bombardment and to micro-manipulation under high-powered microscopes. The delicacy of the work can be gauged from the fact that measurements of the individual lines forming the circuits are discussed in terms of the angstrom unit – one hundred millionth of a centimetre.

The methods of making chips are still developing rapidly as leaders in the field investigate new ways of producing almost unimaginably thin lines. Lithographic processes, contact printing, projection printing, ultraviolet projection, electron-beam lithography and X-ray lithography are all being matched against each other.

The integrated circuits, as the end-products are called, are already used in digital watches, hearing aids, washing machines, cookers, microwave ovens and motor cars. Their spread throughout industrialized countries is likely to be huge since in addition to their obvious advantages they can be mass-produced and their cost

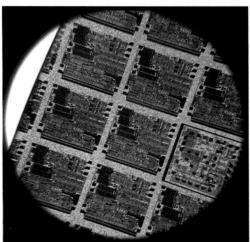

is likely to fall quickly. Just as steam and then electricity took over much of the work done by the human body, integrated circuits are already performing many of the functions for which the human brain was previously required.

Different stages in silicon chip production.

Above: *A silicon crystal (average diameter 60 mm) is sliced into wafers.*

Centre: *A detail from one wafer showing the individual chips assembled; 5 mm squares of complex electronic circuitry.*

Opposite: *One corner from a single chip.*

Below: *The end-product: a single board computer based on an integrated circuit of sealed chips.*

Index and Acknowledgments

The photographs in this book were supplied
and are reproduced by kind permission of
the following:

Aerofilms: 80
Heather Angel: 38
Ardea Photographics: 33 (Valerie Taylor)
Paul Brierley: 1, 27, 31, 82, 83 above, 84, 93,
   94–5, 95
J. Allan Cash: 34 below
John Cleare: 24, 25
Bruce Coleman Ltd: 11 (Bill Brooks); 18–19,
   36 above (Charlie Ott); 32–3 (Bill Wood);
   34 above (Jeff Foott); 36 below, 37 above
   left (Jane Burton); 44 above (Jan and Des
   Bartlett); 45 above (Kim Taylor); 45 below
   (John Pearson); 63 (Michael Freeman)
Colour Library International: 20, 62
Ed Cooper: endpapers, 9
Daily Telegraph Colour Library: 49 below
   (P. Thurston); 92 (A. Howarth)
Photo Desjeux: 17
Douglas Dickins: 57, 58 below, 59, 68, 72–3
Explorer: 10 (Wolf Winter); 28 below
   (C. Delu)
Explorer/Fiore: 8
Fiore: 16–17
Michael Freeman: 12
Giraudon: 79
Susan Griggs: 55; 73, 74, 74–5 (Adam
   Woolfitt); 77 (Julian Calder)
Sonia Halliday: 61, 68–9, 78 (Jane Taylor)
Robert Harding Associates: 2–3, 14,
   14–15 (Geoff Renner); 52 (Sassoon)
John Hillelson: 50–1, 90 (René
   Burri/Magnum)
Alan Hutchison Library: 6–7, 28 above
Jacana Scientific: 37 below (Michel Viard);
   44 below (Massart); 46, 46–7; 48 (Ziesler)
Frank W. Lane: 39 below right, 47 above
   and below
Tony Morrison: 53
NASA: 88, 89, 91
Natural Science Photos: 39 above (P.H.
   Ward)
Nuridsany et Pérennou: 30, 39 below left,
   42–3
Oxford Scientific Films: 40, 40–1 (Stephen
   Dalton)
Photri: 26, 56, 67
Picturepoint: 22–3, 23
Science Photo Library: 4–5 (Dr D. Gorham,
   Dr I. Hutchings); 49 above
John S. Shelton: 22, 29
Solarfilm H.F.: 18
Tony Stone Associates: 64, 76
Vautier, Decool: 54–5
Victoria and Albert Museum: 65
Vision International: 60–1, 70, 71, 72 (Paolo
   Koch); 84–5 (Steve Herr)
ZEFA: 13, 58 above (R. Halin); 21 (S. Deleu);
   66; 81 (J. Pfaff); 82–3 (Til)

Illustrations: Eugene Fleury (86–7) and
   Elaine Keenan (35)
Picture Research: Anne-Marie Ehrlich